THE EUROPEAN HISTORY SERIES

SERIES EDITOR

KEITH EUBANK

ARTHUR S. LINK

GENERAL EDITOR FOR HISTORY

BRITAIN
1914 – 1945

THE AFTERMATH
OF POWER

BENTLEY BRINKERHOFF
GILBERT

UNIVERSITY OF ILLINOIS AT CHICAGO

HARLAN DAVIDSON, INC.

WHEELING, ILLINOIS 60090-6000

Library of Congress Cataloging-in-Publication Data

Gilbert, Bentley B., 1924–
Britain, 1914–1945 : the aftermath of power / Bentley Brinkerhoff Gilbert.
p.   cm. — (European history series)
Includes bibliographical references (p. 145) and index.
ISBN 0-88295-927-1
1. Great Britain—History—George V, 1910–1936. 2. Great Britain—
History—George VI, 1936–1952. 3. Great Britain—History,
Military—20th century. 4. Great Britain—Economic
conditions—1918–1945. 5. World War, 1914–1918—Great Britain.
6. World War, 1939–1945—Great Britain. I. Title. II. Series:
European history series (Wheeling, Ill.)
DA576.G55   1996
941.083—dc20   95-47623
                                                    CIP

Cover illustration: detail from the Low cartoon, "Very Well, Alone,"
published in the *Evening Standard*, June 18, 1940.
Courtesy The British Library Newspaper Library.

Manufactured in the United States of America
98 97 96 95 1 2 3 4 5 BC

FOREWORD

Now more than ever there is a need for books dealing with significant themes in European history, books offering fresh interpretations of events which continue to affect Europe and the world. The end of the Cold War has changed Europe, and to understand the changes, a knowledge of European history is vital. Although there is no shortage of newspaper stories and television reports about politics and life in Europe today, there is a need for interpretation of these developments as well as background information that neither television nor newspapers can provide. At the same time, scholarly interpretations of European history itself are changing.

A guide to understanding Europe begins with knowledge of its history. To understand European history is also to better understand much of the American past because many of America's deepest roots are in Europe. And in these days of increasingly global economic activity, more American men and women journey to Europe for business as well as personal travel. In both respects, knowledge of European history can deepen one's understanding, experience, and effectiveness.

The European History Series introduces readers to the excitement of European history through concise books about the great events, issues, and personalities of Europe's past. Here are accounts of the powerful political and religious movements which shaped European life in the past and which have influenced events in Europe today. Colorful stories of rogues and heroines, tyrants, rebels, fanatics, generals, statesmen, kings, queens, emperors, and ordinary people are contained in these concise studies of major themes and problems in European history.

Each volume in the series examines an issue, event, or era which posed a problem of interpretation for historians. The chosen topics are neither obscure nor narrow. These books are neither historiographical essays, nor substitutes for textbooks,

nor monographs with endless numbers of footnotes. Much
thought and care have been given to their writing style to avoid
academic jargon and overspecialized focus. Authors of the
European History Series have been selected not only for their
recognized scholarship but also for their ability to write for the
general reader. Using primary and secondary sources in their
writing, these authors bring alive the great moments in European history rather than simply cram factual material into the
pages of their books. The authors combine more in-depth interpretation than is found in the usual survey accounts with syn-
thesis of the finest scholarly works, but, above all, they seek to
write absorbing historical narrative.

Each volume contains a bibliographical essay which introduces
readers to the most significant works dealing with their subject.
These are works that are generally available in American public
and college libraries. It is hoped that the bibliographical essays
will enable readers to follow their interests in further reading
about particular pieces of the fascinating European past described in this series.

Keith Eubank
Series Editor

CONTENTS

PEACE AND FUTURE CANNON FODDER

The Tiger: "Curious! I seem to hear a child weeping!"

Two political cartoons: Left, published in the *Daily Herald*, on May 17, 1919, ten days after Germany received the draft of what became the Treaty of Versailles. Shows, from left, Lloyd George, Victor Orlando (Italy), Georges Clemenceau, "The Tiger," and Woodrow Wilson. The child weeping is in the 1940 class of recruits; a copy of the treaty is at his feet. Below is the famous David Low cartoon of June 18, 1940, from the *Evening Standard*, on the day France asked for an armistice. Courtesy The British Library Newspaper Library

June 18, 1940   "VERY WELL, ALONE"   (Copyright in All Countries)

PREFACE

Rather than a narrative history, this essay is an interpretive discussion of prevailing trends in Britain between 1914 and 1945. It analyzes the decline of Britain's place and power in international affairs, which may be ascribed largely to its decline in economic efficiency. The underlying causes of Britain's diminished potency stemmed from wounds of the First World War (the Great War) that were left untreated, and worse even unrecognized, in the 1920s and 1930s, although the symptoms, as in the banking crisis of 1931, were readily apparent. Hence, Britain continued to behave as a first-class power, determining policy toward Nazi Germany in the years after 1936 and forcing a reluctant France into a war in 1939 for which both nations were tragically unprepared.

It follows that this study does not attempt to include all major events of the period. Many occurrences regarded as hugely important in their time have been omitted. For example, I have not looked at Britain's campaign in Africa between 1940 and 1943. I do not question the importance of the battle in the desert as a factor in the revival of British morale. El Alamein was the first clearcut victory on land for British arms. But still, the war and Britain's survival were decided elsewhere. More important here, the centerpiece of the welfare state, the National Health Service, was beginning to take shape in Britain's wartime emergency medical scheme. For the future of Britain this development would be of great significance.

Generally then, the intent in this study of the period 1914 to 1945 has been to look forward, to examine the result, to ask how Britain came to be what it was in 1945, rather than to investigate what was its state in 1914, as the historian does most often. Usually, I have tried to signal the reader that some apparently inconsequential occurrence, for example, the absorption of the Royal Naval Air Service into the Royal Air Force, would be of great importance for the future. I have slighted discussion of the Labour governments, mostly because the Labour party in office did little except to assure the British voter of its respectability. On the other hand, the discussion encompasses the sad story of trade unionism in the interwar period, which had its obvious repercussions in 1945.

On a more cheerful note, while Britain is no longer the world's policeman, nor the world's conscience, it would be flying in the face of facts to assert that Britain's citizens today are not more affluent, better housed, better fed and physically more comfortable than they were at the beginning of the century. It is just possible that they also are happier.

Bentley Brinkerhoff Gilbert
University of Illinois at Chicago

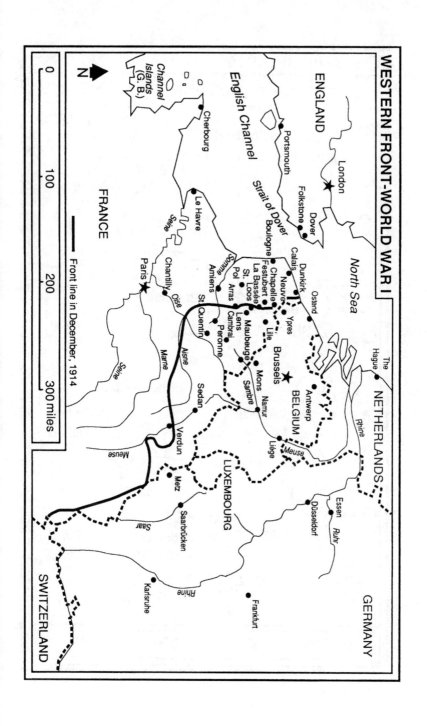

The Balkans, 1914

AUSTRIA-HUNGARY

N

RUSSIA

★ Budapest

HUNGARY

Danube

TRANSYLVANIA

ROMANIA

(AUSTRIA)
Bosnia

★ Belgrade

Bucharest ★

Constanza

● Sarajevo

SERBIA

River

Nish ●

Sofia ★

Black Sea

MONTENEGRO

BULGARIA

MACEDONIA

Tirané ★

Monastir ●

Constantinople ●

Adriatic Sea

Salonika ●

Gallipoli Peninsula

Sea of Marmora

ALBANIA

LEMNOS

ITALY

Straits of Dardanelles

TURKEY

GREECE

Smyrna ●

Ionian Sea

Athens ★

Aegean Sea

| 0 miles | 150 | 300 | 450 |

Europe, Pre-World War II, 1935–1939

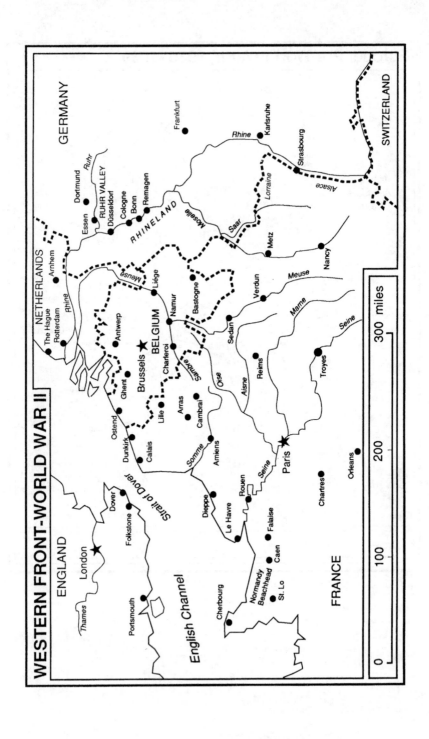

1 / THE GREAT WAR,
THE FIRST YEAR

WHY WAR NOW, AND WHY SO QUICKLY?

At an hour before midnight on the comfortably warm evening of August 4, 1914, Winston Churchill opened the window of his office at the Admiralty facing the Mall. From the west toward Buckingham Palace drifted the sound of an immense crowd singing "God Save the King." Presently, over the chorus came the stroke of Big Ben announcing the eleventh hour. Turning to a clerk Churchill ordered the signal "Commence hostilities against Germany" made to all ships and stations of the Royal Navy. With these four words Britain entered the Great War.

In sharp contrast to the events surrounding the outbreak of the Second World War, August 1914 found the British public and most of the political world stunned, and then, on the whole, jubilant. The war had erupted without warning. For months the attention of both government and press had been concentrated upon Irish Home Rule. Cabinet meetings during July had been devoted entirely to the crisis in Ulster. Only on July 27, just eight days before the war began, had foreign secretary Sir Edward Grey warned his colleagues of the grave developments in Europe. Even at that time many ministers felt that a war in Europe, if it occurred, was not Britain's affair. That Germany should attack France because Austria attacked Serbia was a non sequitur; that Britain should therefore attack Germany was almost incomprehensible. When Prussia and its allies had gone to war with France only a little more than a generation earlier in 1870, few had suggested British involvement. In fact British public opinion in 1870 had largely supported the Germans. And even more ironically, in the spring of 1914 relations between Britain and its North Sea neighbor, after a serious crisis over Morocco in 1911 which

1

had frightened politicians in both countries, were better than they had been in years.

The ethical and legal arguments for Britain's involvement in a continental quarrel over issues which seemed remote were given by Sir Edward Grey in a speech to the House of Commons on the afternoon of Monday, August 3, 1914. Germany, he said, without warning and in defiance of its own treaty commitments, had invaded its Belgian neighbor to the west. Belgium was recognized by treaty as totally neutral and was allied with none of the belligerent powers. Germany, announced Grey, had committed this breach of international morality solely for its own convenience inasmuch as the Belgian territory lay across the shortest route to France. But most important, although Britain had no written obligation to any of the major European powers, the nation was in fact committed by an 1839 treaty to defend Belgian neutrality, as were all of the major European nations including Germany.

By invading Belgium Germany thus had flouted both human decency and international law. Britain was bound therefore, both legally and morally, to aid Belgium. The King of the Belgians conveniently issued an appeal for military support at the moment Grey was speaking.

All that Sir Edward Grey told the House of Commons about the British obligation to Belgium was perfectly true. There was no question that the German attack on Belgium was ruthless and unprovoked, and in subsequent days the German army behaved toward the Belgians with unapologetic harshness. However, the Foreign Secretary was less emphatic when admitting that there also existed a British understanding with France to help defend the French seacoast should the German navy come down the English Channel. Grey deliberately added that the French had been warned that fulfillment of this understanding depended upon the consent of Parliament. But he did not explain to the House that Britain's commitment to France, as well as his own, went far deeper. He did not reveal that only the day before, August 2, in the first Cabinet meeting of two on that Sunday, he had threatened to resign unless Britain threw its support behind France, whether or not the Germans invaded Belgium. Prime Minister Herbert Asquith seems to have said nothing at the time but wrote later that day that he would have followed his Foreign Secretary. Thus the Liberal government would have broken up. Parliament did not know that it was being invited to consent to a decision that the Cabinet had already made.

The story of Britain's guarantee of French security against Germany, the so-called *Entente* (understanding), has commanded a good deal of attention in recent years and need not be a part of this essay. For a generation scholars connected the genesis of *Entente* with the secret clauses of the Anglo-French treaty of 1904 in which Britain promised to support a French claim to a position in Morocco similar to the unofficial protectorate status held by Britain in Egypt. Indeed older history books refer to the "signing" of the *Entente* in 1904.

There was an *Entente*, but it did not refer to Morocco, it was never actually signed, and while it began with highly secret but low-level military conversations in 1905, it really did not come into full bloom until after the sinister Agadir crisis in 1911. This British-French understanding proceeded from several sources: a long-standing anti-Germanism among officials at the British Foreign Office, Director of Military Operations General Henry Wilson's warm regard for France, and newspaper warnings about the rapid growth of the German navy, among others. But above all it grew from the post–Agadir conviction of Cabinet leaders, the Prime Minister, the Foreign Secretary, the Lord Chancellor, R. B. Haldane, and the Chancellor of the Exchequer, David Lloyd George (a reported pacifist), that Britain, even consulting only its own interests, could not allow Germany to defeat and dismember France a second time in the way it had done in the Franco-Prussian War, 1870–71. The danger to Britain, let alone other nations, of a France reduced to a third-class power and a Europe dominated by an armed and efficient, but restless and unstable Germany was simply too great. What would the naval race be like then? What would become of the British Empire, not to mention the British Isles? The ramifications were horrifying. A second premise of Britain's commitment to France, narrower but no less pressing than the first, was that without Britain's help the Germans would defeat France again quickly. They would "walk through the French army like partridges" predicted Herbert, Lord Kitchener, Britain's senior Field Marshal on active duty.

All of this, it must be emphasized, ignored the integrity of Belgium and proceeded only incidentally from any British admiration for France. Britain's need to protect France was solely a function of its own vital interests. In older times it would have been styled the maintenance of the balance of power.

Hence it was the unwritten commitment to France rather than the treaty obligation to Belgium that dictated Britain's immediate declaration of war against Germany in 1914. But more important for this essay, that commitment also determined British military strategy in the war. Oddly, by requiring a concentration on the front in France, Britain gave up its traditional strategy of commanding the sea to attack a continental power at its periphery, the "blue water strategy." As France became the senior partner in the alliance, Britain's task was to help defend it rather than to defeat Germany. The two purposes, it would be proven again and again, were not the same thing.

In pursuit of the diplomatic and military imperatives it used as a guide for policy, the British nation undertook a prodigious mobilization of its manufacturing and mineral resources, of its workforce, and, above all, of its wealth. None of this had been foreseen, let alone planned, before the war, but would become critical. The term had not yet appeared, but in 1914 Britain unwittingly, although innocently and enthusiastically, embarked upon "total war."

It is probably fair to say that for Britain the First World War truly was, as it was customarily called until 1939, the Great War. Although the nation's battle casualties were proportionally somewhat smaller than were France's or Germany's, and while British land was not violated as was French or Belgian territory, in a peculiar way more of what Britain essentially was, or saw itself to be, was destroyed. After the war the Empire (dominions outside of the British Isles) ceased to be a glory and became a burden. Internationally Britain was no longer a creditor but a debtor, while domestically the Treasury and the taxpayer were forced to carry the interest cost of internal borrowing ten times larger than in 1914. Economically the markets for its largest exports, those that had brought one hundred years of growth and upon which the industrial revolution had been built, coal, textiles, steel, and ships, had been diminished or stolen. British economic preeminence, and with it Britain's ability to intervene at will in world affairs, had disappeared. Britain's position as the peacemaker and policeman of the world ended with the First World War. The nation's leaders understood this quickly, although the formal dignity was not surrendered until after the second war.

More troublesome to delineate, although easily recognizable and in the long run the most devastating, was the destruction of the liberal creed of inevitable political and economic progress by which the nation lived. Quaintly or innocently, in the decades before the war, there seemed to exist a sense of purpose in the affairs of the country in which nearly all British citizens believed: their world was getting better and would continue to do so. Such evidence to the contrary as turned up, the discovery in the years around the turn of the twentieth century of widespread poverty and of a deteriorating physical condition among working classes in the cities, did not mean that the assumption of progress was incorrect, only that something needed to be fixed. The words "Land of Hope and Glory" were not ironic in those days—they meant something.

Belief in the comforting doctrine of moral and physical progress, with overtones of the natural superiority of British civilization, provided the logic of imperialism on one hand and the singular orderliness and patriotism of the nation's citizens on the other. For nearly three-quarters of a century it had been a characteristic of Victorian Britain that foreigners could only marvel at or despise. From it proceeded the remarkable civility of politics. It allowed the trade union movement and political parties not to resist, but rather to ignore, the doctrines of socialism. To be sure the famous study by George Dangerfield, *The Strange Death of Liberal England*, and a good many subsequent works, have suggested that this tolerant public consensus had begun to break down in the last years before the war. There is unquestionably much evidence of a menacing violence in public life in the decade before the war that seemed to be alien to British traditions. Yet, when the August 1914 crisis appeared, all the intractable issues evaporated still unresolved, and insurgents in Ireland and in trade unions, who a few days earlier had been contemplating rebellion, suddenly became patriots. In a crisis, the old beliefs were so far unshaken.

Generalizations in scholarly history are always dangerous and can be chipped at in detail, but are not invariably wrong and are sometimes necessary. Old-fashioned liberalism indeed did die in the First World War, accompanying to the grave belief in individual betterment and political and economic progress. Principle was replaced by dogmatism. The comfortable assurance that progress lay in the refinement of existing institutions was swept away by a wave of nostalgia for the better days before 1914, the opposite of progress. Earnestness became a joke and was replaced by cynicism.

Still, twenty-one years later war came again to a nation that thought it had learned its lesson. In 1939 Britain embarked upon a more dangerous and far more necessary war not as a joyous crusade but as a grim and unpleasant task. No clearcut principle was involved here; the rights of small nations already had been sacrificed attempting to prevent the war. Instead, the British nation's very survival was at stake. These topics, the two wars and the story of the decades between them during which Britain struggled first to adjust to the consequences of one war and then to unite itself in preparation for a second, provide the central theme of this study.

PLANNING FOR WAR

Not even the entire Cabinet was aware of Britain's secret commitments to France until the end of 1911. This understanding dictated not only the quick declaration of war in the first week of August 1914 but the military strategy that followed it. At the height of Agadir, on August 23, 1911, the Prime Minister, Herbert Asquith, had summoned a meeting of the Committee of Imperial Defence (C.I.D.) to consider in general terms what Britain should do in the event of a German attack upon France and specifically to discover the army's and the navy's plans to meet such an attack. Although for two centuries British military plans had assumed that the nation would not even try to put an army comparable to continental forces into the field, that its contribution instead would be the navy and money, one soldier, Brigadier General Henry H. Wilson, the Director of Military Operations, who dominated the meeting, thought otherwise.

With his considerable Irish eloquence, Wilson convinced the Cabinet members present, including several senior politicians who had not attended a C.I.D. meeting before, that Britain must declare war and mobilize its regular army at the same time as the French. Unlike 1870, he predicted, a German attack upon France would come through Belgium. Wilson assured the C.I.D. that as the Germans would need to divide their army, the German force in Belgium would be no larger than that of the French. Each side would be able to field about forty divisions on the Belgian front. Thus, explained General Wilson, the Cabinet must make plans for the prompt dispatch of the six divisions of the already organized British Expeditionary Force (B.E.F.) to the Belgian-French border between Maubeuge and Mons. Wilson was sure the Germans would remain to the south and east of the line of the Sambre-Meuse rivers, and because the two sides would be about equal in size, the relatively small, but highly trained B.E.F. appearing on the German right flank would decide the course of the war.

There were two farreaching results of this 1911 C.I.D. meeting. The conclusions reached at the meeting became the basis for all there was of forward planning for war by the British government. Britain would not allow France to be overrun again, but had to save it. General Wilson had shown that the British army would ensure a German defeat along the Belgian-French border. The second result was the promotion, two months afterwards, of Winston Churchill to the Admiralty in order to force the navy to prepare plans for the transport of the B.E.F.

In a series of meetings throughout the autumn of 1911 and into 1912, though distracted by the beginnings of Ulster unrest, the full Cabinet gradually was informed of the extent of British commitments to France. Simultaneously, Winston Churchill, the new First Lord of the Admiralty, ordered the navy to plan for the transportation of the B.E.F. Railway timetables and logistical preparations for army mobilization were likewise ordered to proceed. Finally, in the spring and summer of 1912, in the face of Germany's announcement of a huge increase in the strength of its Imperial navy (so that Germany could have, as the Emperor had put it in a speech in Hamburg soon after Agadir, "her place in the sun"), Britain began deployment of the most powerful units of its Royal Navy in the North Sea. All modern battleships were withdrawn from the Mediterranean Sea. At the same time, despite the lack of any written agreement between Britain and France, the French fleet departed from its bases in the English Channel, its traditional home ports since the days of Louis XIV, and concentrated in the south of France at Toulon. The two navies, in effect, had exchanged places. The most important consequence of these movements, which left the northern French ports defenseless, was that Britain agreed informally to guard the French Channel coast against the powerful German navy in the event of war between Germany and France. Although there was still nothing on paper, the fleet movements caused, in reality, a defensive alliance. Prime Minister Herbert Asquith remarks sadly in his book *The Genesis of the War* that these naval dispositions made Britain's entrance into the conflict in 1914 virtually inescapable. Britain had committed itself not legally but morally to the defense of France.

Hence in the months after the Agadir crisis, between August 1911 and July 1912, the decisions that would confront the Cabinet in case of a German attack upon France were made. The question of war became no longer "if," but "when." Whether or not France was a comfortable friend in Europe, let alone in Africa, became irrelevant. Historically France certainly was not. But Britain could never, in its own interest, allow France to be destroyed.

Given the situation there could be no hesitation on Britain's part in 1914. Mobilization of the fleet and army began immediately without even Cabinet, not to mention parliamentary, consent; in the case of the navy mobilization began on Winston Churchill's own initiative, and for the army with a simple manuscript note from Prime Minister Asquith to the Director of Military Operations, General Wilson. The consequences of these seemingly minor decisions, taken hastily over the crowded weekend of Friday, July 31 to Monday August 3, 1914, are of such gigantic importance for the thesis of this study that they must be recapitulated here. First Britain committed itself to war because of determinations made three years earlier over the Agadir crisis in an entirely different diplomatic context. In 1911 Germany's intrusion into French Morocco had threatened the integrity of the French empire, a matter of some concern for Britain. But the 1914 war erupted as a repercussion of the assassination in the Balkan province of Bosnia-Hercegovina of the Austrian heir to the throne over concerns that few Britons understood or cared about. The affair hardly involved Britain, but it did involve France, whom Britain had promised to defend. And so Britain abandoned its century-old policy of isolation not only without public debate but virtually without Cabinet consideration.

In the simplest terms, due to its diplomatic obligations, Britain set into motion military preparations for war without arrangements for the support and supplies necessary for their execution. For example, it had been agreed secretly in 1911 that the six divisions of the B.E.F. should go to the continent to secure the left flank of the French army. But when the fighting started the question arose at once whether six divisions would be enough. This brought up larger questions that had unbelievably occurred to no one thus far: In the end what ought the British contribution to be? Ought not Britain raise a mass army like France and Germany? But this possibility raised another problem. A mass army entailed the creation of a mass armament industry to supply it. Slow to react, the government allowed a year of fighting to elapse, with many soldiers killed because of a shortage of weapons and ammunition, before taking in hand the mobilization of Britain's ample industrial resources. As someone observed on another occasion, it seems that Britain in 1914 abandoned diplomatic isolation and the security that went with it, to involve itself in a mammoth European war in a fit of "absence of mind."

The second devastating consequence of the determination to go to war unprepared on August 4, 1914, was that Britain deployed in Europe a military force more suited to the diplomatic-imperial needs of the nineteenth century. The army was much improved as a result of reforms begun in 1906, but it was nevertheless a force trained, organized, and equipped to fight colonial wars. Naval plans, so far as they existed, proceeded from

Admiralty standing orders. The navy would in descending order defend the United Kingdom, sweep enemy commerce from the sea, convoy the army to the point of attack, and engage the enemy fleet in battle. The Royal Navy was still Nelson's navy.

Hence Britain's armed forces, well-trained and equipped as they were, found themselves almost totally unprepared for the modern war thrust upon them in August 1914. The army had excellent rifles but few machine guns and absolutely no modern heavy artillery. The navy comfortably outnumbered the Germans in battleships, but had far too few destroyers and possessed not one usable submarine mine. Neither force had any schemes for expansion beyond the existing reserves.

For all its bold diplomacy, Britain had no strategic plan. How, in fact, would Germany be fought? Admiralty thinking—"planning" would be too strong a word—remained eighteenth-century: carry the war into the Baltic, seize offshore islands, and land troops on the German coast. The threat of German submarines, sea mines, and railroads was ignored. Conclusions, it was assumed, would be tried in a grand line-of-battle engagement. The army had only one battle plan, General Wilson's, and it was based on the misconception that Britain could fight a continental land war.

For many years after the Great War military historians wondered why the tiny B.E.F. had deployed between Maubeuge and Mons, which turned out to be not on the German flank, but directly in the path of its two strongest armies. Neither Field Marshal Herbert Kitchener, soon to be appointed Secretary of State for War, nor Sir John French, Commander of the B.E.F., approved of the design. Both felt the British should concentrate further west, perhaps at Amiens. French suggested an expedition to Antwerp. At the great War Councils on August 5 and 6, 1914, when the Cabinet leaders and the senior generals assembled to determine, now that the nation had declared war, what in fact it should do, the meeting was dominated once again by Henry Wilson, who favored the plan. German intentions remained unclear, but loading arrangements and railway timetables dictated Maubeuge, and the British were bound to conform to the French army's plans. That settled the matter. Not surprisingly, about one-half of the original B.E.F. were casualties by the end of 1914.

Britain entered the Great War saddled with an enormous disparity between ends and means. Britain's goal was to support France and to prevent German hegemony in Europe. The declaration of hostilities had been nearly automatic. But the government had given almost no sustained thought on how or where its army and navy would give effect to these diplomatic decisions. Much of the story of the First World War must be therefore the unhappy account of Britain's struggle to make good upon the commitments entered into in August 1914. The problems were enormous: how could Britain recruit and arm a mass army, and how could Germany be most usefully attacked? Perhaps more alarming, how could a nation unused to war and numbing casualties be kept from forcing a compromise peace? It is depressing to record that twenty-five years later Britain again entered a war against Germany even less prepared militarily to fulfill the diplomatic promises it had once made. At that time the consequence for the nation was near disaster.

THE WAR AT HOME

In the first year of the Great War, a politician's usual defense against charges of lack of preparation for the adventure upon which Britain had embarked so lightly was that the war would be short. It would be over before the nation could train and arm huge continental-sized armies. On the whole, the war would have to be fought with the resources at hand. Not only the political world believed this. Tens of thousands who rushed to join the forces lest the war end before they reached the front agreed. For too many months this dangerous illusion remained current among many who should have known better. For some it lasted until the Battle of Loos at the end of September 1915.

Nonetheless, long before, in August 1914 only days after the war began, the Cabinet allowed itself to be committed to the mobilization of a mass (eventually seventy-division) army to be enlisted for three years. Unbelievably, this astonishing decision was taken alone by the newly appointed Secretary of State for War, Lord Kitchener, and accepted by the Cabinet in utter silence. Pertinent questions such as how this huge army would be raised, armed, and paid for were not asked.

The two overriding political themes in the history of the First World War arose from Kitchener's unilateral decision on a mass army in August 1914. The first was the search for weapons, and the second was the search for men (military conscription). From the government's point of view, the story of the years from August 1914 to November 1918 fell into these two well-defined periods. In the first period, from the beginning of the war until the end of 1915, the Asquith administration sought frantically, but in the end successfully, to buy or produce the hardware of modern battle. This was a war of munitions, an "engineers' war" announced David Lloyd George, who became head of the newly created Ministry of Munitions in May 1915. Rather quickly the munitions program proved to be a great success. When the Ministry of Munitions was formally established in June of 1915, for example, Britain was producing about 150,000 rounds of artillery ammunition of all sizes per week. But the War Office was unable to supply even the minimal ration of seventeen rounds per day of eighteen-pound shells to its most widely used field gun. By March of 1916 production was 600,000 per week and ammunition for eighteen-pounders was unrationed. Britain was not only able to supply itself but to provide huge quantities of weapons and ammunition for Russia. Moreover, Lloyd George's energetic and highly visible leadership in the resolution of the munitions crisis put him into competition with Asquith for the position of Prime Minister. In December 1916 Lloyd George would replace Asquith as head of the government.

But the demand for munitions to supply Kitchener's massive new army required that the British government spend money on a scale unimagined even two years before. Despite increases in income taxes to the then unheard of rate of 25 percent, nearly three-quarters of the cost of the war had to be covered by borrowing. Britain's internal indebtedness increased by a factor of ten during the Great War.

Perhaps more disastrous, Britain accumulated in the United States an additional external debt of about ten billion dollars. These loans were made partly as guarantees for French, Italian, and Russian borrowing as well as for the purchase of American weapons and ammunition for the new British armies. In January 1915 Lloyd George signed a contract for the British government with the J. P. Morgan Bank in the United States, which agreed to act both as the purchasing agent for arms and as the lead bank in the syndications to raise funds to pay for them. The terms indicated that at that time the amount of money Britain expected to spend in America would be small. However, two years later, purchases of arms in the United States and Canada, plus the guarantee of foreign (French, Italian, and Russian) loans had not only used up the London banking system's huge supply of dollars, but had forced the government to borrow about three billion dollars from American banks (Reginald McKenna, Chancellor of the Exchequer, usually expressed Britain's financial needs in the United States as "£2,000,000, i.e. $9,600,000 per day"). When the United States entered the war, on April 6, 1917, and the U.S. government bought the British loans held by private institutions in America, Britain was completely dependent upon creditors, chiefly the United States, to pay its bills abroad. By international standards it was, as it would be again in the spring of 1941, technically bankrupt. To this end Britain's unconsidered decision to fight the Great War on European terms came. For a century, and during the wars of the French Revolution and Napoleon, Britain had built its strength by trade. No one had considered what would happen if that trade should be interrupted by war or if the British export industry converted suddenly to war production. Ultimately over one hundred years of accumulated British savings were blown away in fifty-one months.

The purpose of the preceding sections has not been to demonstrate that even honest, patriotic, and indeed intelligent, men are unable to predict the future. Far too many historians of both the First and the Second World Wars have criticized statesmen for making decisions that turned out badly, from which, presumably, one is to infer that the historians might have done better. The point here is that the First World War was a conflict not only unforeseen but unprecedented. It was expected by all nations to be short, as had been the Franco-Prussian and the Russo-Japanese wars, neither of which was a minor nor merciful conflict. Politicians and soldiers envisioned a war of movement with a few large and no doubt bloody battles leading to an armistice and a negotiated peace. The war became instead a war of position and of attrition, a siege war, in which only the killing of men in staggering numbers and the starvation of civilians would produce victory. As has been discussed, it was not a war of distant armies, during which the people at home went about their customary business, such as had occurred even during the desperate Napoleonic war (one need only read the novels of Jane Austen, who lived through it). It was, rather, a war of nations. No one could forget or ignore it. Everyone, men and women alike, had to work or fight.

Finally, for Britain particularly, the war brought an end of an era, in fact of a civilization. The war was a holocaust that burned away not the memory, but the reality of the Victorian age. Its monuments appeared not only in acre upon acre of cemetery crosses in France and Flanders but also, perhaps more poignantly, in the silent mining, textile, and shipyard towns of England, Scotland, and North Ireland with their now smokeless chimneys and shuttered factories.

THE FIGHTING

War, to the soldier, it has been remarked, is a long featureless drama made up of extended periods of exhaustion and boredom interrupted by moments of sheer terror. In the trenches of the First World War this was certainly true. Yet it is also a fact that for Britons at home, the perception of the huge undertaking upon which the nation had embarked moved through a number of well-defined phases. These are important to note because popular attitudes toward the war determined the responses politicians were able to make to the demands of the conflict.

From the declaration of war on August 4 until almost the end of December 1914, the prevailing mood among civilians and soldiers alike was that of exhilaration. The war provided an adventure not to be missed. Over 1,186,000 young men enlisted in these first five months. Arguably the public enthusiasm of this first period could have made possible besides recruits, the necessary political atmosphere for the introduction of conscription, higher taxes, labor controls, and rationing. The occasion was neglected, and all of these unpopular sacrifices had to be made later amid much controversy and at ruinous political cost to the Liberal party and Prime Minister Asquith.

None of this had been foreseen by the government. Why make plans that could not mature for eighteen months when they were sure the war would be over by Christmas? Why consider conscription, as was done briefly by the Cabinet at the end of August, when the army had already more volunteers than it could train or equip?

The excitement disappeared speedily with the beginning of 1915. Very suddenly it was clear not only that the war would not end by Christmas, but that it would not end anytime soon. An early indication of the decline in the martial spirit during the first six months of 1915 appeared in the falling rate of enlistment in the forces coupled, not accidentally, with rising levels of employment, increasing wages, and strikes. Unemployment, which had been expected to increase as the conflict interfered with trade, almost disappeared. The war, in fact, was bringing unexampled prosperity, and with it complacency.

In reality, the situation in France was not good. Although the tiny British army had performed gallantly in holding up the advance of the huge German First Army in August of 1914, in securing the French left flank during the Battle of the Marne in mid-September, and in stabilizing the battleline to the English Channel in November with a bloody battle at Ypres in Belgium, it was already clear to some members of the government that the military were prepared for a different war.

The King's forces in the years since the South African war had been rearmed, retrained, and professionalized. They were excellent marksmen, understood the use of natural cover, and were expert in night infiltration and topography. In 1904 the army had adopted a new, light, quick-firing, highly mobile field artillery gun, the Eighteen Pounder. In every way British forces were perfectly prepared for another South African war. Unfortunately, northern France and Flanders were not the Transvaal, nor did the Imperial German Army resemble the Boer commandos.

By the end of October 1914 it was becoming obvious to some men in the British government, politicians rather than soldiers, that the present war was unlike any since the invention of gunpowder. The weapons of defense, the murderous trinity of barbed wire, machine guns, and heavy artillery capable of high trajectory fire, had achieved almost complete control of the battlefield. Even moderately trained troops in well-constructed trenches protected by barbed wire, which itself was protected by machine guns, all backed by artillery with plenty of ammunition, were almost invulnerable to an attack, however bravely it was conducted. And with continuous battlelines running from the Swiss border to the English Channel, by the end of 1914 there were no flanks to turn.

Thus before it was six months old the war, at least on the Western Front, had evolved into a stalemate similar to the siege warfare of the Middle Ages. In such a conflict the B.E.F.'s mobility, its polished skirmishing expertise and small-unit capabilities, were nearly useless. Worst of all, it had no modern heavy artillery and too little light artillery ammunition. The army had begun the war with what it had believed was a three-year reserve of artillery shells. By the spring of 1915 this was all gone and the inadequate new production had to be rationed to the batteries. On May 9 an attack conducted by General Douglas Haig at Aubers Ridge was beaten back with the British suffering 11,000 casualties in less than an hour when supporting artillery ran out of ammunition. Here lay the beginning of a crisis, first military but then political, that ended almost precisely nineteen months later on December 7, 1916, with the destruction of the government of Herbert Henry Asquith as well as of the creed of the British Liberal party.

2 / THE WAR, 1915

DARDANELLES-GALLIPOLI

By the end of 1914, the clear evidence of stalemate on the Western Front led military and political leaders of all nations toward consideration of alternative theaters of operation. The Germans themselves used 1915 to concentrate in the East against Russia. The British began to consider an attack against Austria-Hungary in the Balkans or against some part of Turkey, which had joined the Central Powers (Germany and Austria-Hungary) on October 29, 1914. Early in November a small war committee of Asquith's Cabinet opened a leisurely discussion of the options either of an offensive against the Sultan's capital of Constantinople or of a landing somewhere in the Adriatic or the Aegean Sea to help Serbia in its battle against Austria.

These unhurried conversations suddenly became crisis planning in the first days of January 1915, with a series of frantic telegrams from Russia pleading for an immediate British operation against Turkey to relieve dangerous pressure upon the Czar's armies in the Caucasus Mountains. With very little consideration of alternatives, the committee, now styled the War Council, settled, at the urging of Winston Churchill, upon an attack on Constantinople, using battleships of the Royal Navy to force the Straits of Dardanelles. Once the ships had emerged from the straits into the Sea of Marmora, Churchill argued, the city itself could be brought under naval gunfire, the Sultan would have to flee his seat of power, Turkey would probably leave the war, and a warm-water supply route to Russia, now badly wounded, would be open.

The Dardanelles-Gallipoli campaign occupied Britain throughout the whole of 1915. Few military operations have promised so great a return for so small an investment and few have begun with such high hopes and so little planning. The campaign's failure convinced Bulgaria to enter the war on the side of Germany (as the certain victor) which resulted in the collapse of Serbia and disastrous British defeats at the hand of the Turks in Mesopotamia (now Iraq). By isolating Russia from the West, the failed campaign certainly hastened, if it did not cause, the Russian Revolution. For Britain, the disastrous repulse in the Eastern Mediterranean meant that the nation's military effort was now tied irrevocably to the bloody Western Front. Politically, it helped to destroy the last single party Liberal government in May 1915. It nearly ended the political career of Winston Churchill. Success in the Dardanelles-Gallipoli, in effect, could have changed the course of the war and perhaps of twentieth-century history. Its failure ensured that the war would be long, with an Allied victory by no means certain.

The Dardanelles-Gallipoli naval and military story can be told quickly. The overriding problem for the government was the availability of ground troops. Ships, after all, might be able to force the Straits of Dardanelles and cause the surrender of Constantinople, but they could not occupy the city. And few experienced soldiers were available for occupation. In the first weeks of 1915 Britain was still in the process of bringing home the regular army units from the Empire, and the masses of young men who had enlisted in the last five months of 1914 were as yet untrained and, to a frightening extent, unarmed. Soldiers for an operation against Turkey therefore would have to come from the B.E.F. in France, a plan stubbornly resisted by the military command in both France and London. In the War Council, Lord Kitchener, Secretary of State for War, hesitated and dithered. Sometimes he would promise troops would be available "when needed." On other occasions he would mumble that no troops were ready "now." Meanwhile, Winston Churchill asked the naval Commander in Chief in the Mediterranean, Admiral S. H. Carden, for an estimate of the possibility of forcing the Straits with battleships alone. After some hesitation Carden replied that his ships could, with prolonged bombardment, reduce the stone forts guarding the approaches to Constantinople. On January 28, 1915, the War Council approved the plan. Nothing was said about soldiers. On all sides it was assumed that land forces would be available sometime later. If the forts proved to be too strong, the navy could announce that the whole exercise was simply another demonstration and withdraw. (The navy already had bombarded the outer forts shortly after Turkey declared war.) On these slender premises, better styled as suppositions, the naval attack began on February 19, with an Allied Fleet of fourteen old British battleships, one modern battle cruiser, and four old French battleships.

During the first two weeks the attack proceeded smoothly. The forts at the tip of the Gallipoli peninsula, Cape Hellas, were silenced, and marines, who landed to blow up any remaining ordnance, found them deserted. By the beginning of March the navy, the government, and above all Winston Churchill, were jubilant, and the good news was released to the press. As the fleet prepared to move into the narrow straits to begin the systematic destruction of the inner forts, newspapers began to predict the imminent capture of Constantinople, the surrender of Turkey, and the opening of the Balkans to the Allies. The price of wheat dropped on the Chicago Board of Trade in the anticipation of renewed Russian exports. Greece, which had been resisting Allied diplomatic efforts, suddenly appeared eager to join the war against Turkey.

Within the confining straits, submarine mines, not the forts, were expected to be a problem, but the fleet had minesweepers available, and sweeping had begun even before the outer forts were fully secure. On March 7 Allied battleships entered the narrow waters. For ten days everything went well. One by one the Turkish forts, old fashioned in design and mounting out-of-date guns, were destroyed. Minesweepers were constantly busy ahead of the ships moving up the channel. But here the Allied force encountered the difficulty that would soon destroy the whole enterprise. As Turkish fortresses were reduced, the Turks began to deploy field guns in boulder-strewn ravines that creased the shoreline on either side of the channel. The fire of these light guns presented no danger to the heavily armored battleships, but a hit on one of the minesweepers, most of them simply fishing trawlers, could easily be fatal. Still worse the warships found it almost impossible to engage the field batteries. The guns could be hidden behind rocks and in folds in the terrain where the flat trajectory fire of naval guns could not reach them. If found, the Turks simply moved them. As a consequence, sweeping for submarine mines too often was accomplished hastily and incompletely.

The end came quickly. At 1:54 P.M. on March 18 the French battleship *Bouvet* struck a mine about six miles into the channel and about 2,000 yards off the eastern shore in an area that had been signalled clear. She sank with 600 men. As it was uncertain whether *Bouvet* had been hit by a mine, a torpedo, or an unexpected heavy projectile, the firing continued. Then between 4:00 and 6:00 P.M. three British battleships struck mines in the same area. That evening the naval commander ordered the attack cancelled and signalled his decision to London. The naval penetration of the straits could not continue until the shores were cleared of light artillery. Thus it became clear that an army was needed, and no troops were available. The naval attack had lasted precisely four weeks. Churchill's enthusiasm had ensured that the Turks were warned of British plans in ample detail by British newspapers. This bombardment was no demonstration. The Allied objective was Constantinople and after that, an entry into the Balkans.

The disastrous and bloody Gallipoli operation was a result of the War Council's lack of foresight in planning the naval penetration. The Turkish deployment of field guns had been anticipated, but their importance was waved aside by Churchill whose eagerness to make the attack on Constantinople must be counted as a factor in the improvised character of the entire operation. Field guns, after all, could not harm battleships. The vulnerability of the minesweepers had not been taken into account, however.

Churchill, it should be noted, says very little about minesweeping in his extensive and generally excellent account of Dardanelles-Gallipoli in the second volume of *The World Crisis*, except to observe that it was badly done. Pointedly he does not explain why it was badly done.

The assembly of an Allied army to occupy the Gallipoli peninsula took six weeks, a period of time which was, the German commander of the Turks noted in his memoirs, just enough to prepare the peninsula's defense. Allied landings thus began on April 25 with a scratch force of 35,000 coming ashore at Cape

Hellas, and a raw unit of the Australian and New Zealand Army Corps (ANZACs) landing at Gaba Tepe about fifteen miles further north on the western coast. While the British and ANZAC forces had the benefit of tactical surprise in terms of landing plans, they used this advantage badly and for practical purposes never got off the original beaches, while the Turks commanded the rocky central highlands of the narrow peninsula. The conquest of Gallipoli, which, with better planning, could have been accomplished in a matter of weeks at the beginning of March 1915, proved to be impossible by the end of April.

There is no need to tell in detail the grim story of the bloody Gallipoli campaign, which occupied the rest of the year of 1915. The last troops were withdrawn on January 9, 1916, without loss. The evacuation, one could remark, was the only phase of the Allied operation handled efficiently. In all, 410,000 soldiers, from Britain and the Empire, and 70,000 French, were engaged in the Gallipoli campaign. Approximately half this number became casualties, many thousands from sickness, since logistical support was unbelievably difficult, with fresh water unavailable and sanitation impossible. The Turkish position was worse, but the Turks held on. It was not their only victory in the Great War, but it was their most important.

The effects of the Gallipoli failure were devastating to the Allied cause. On October 11, 1915, Bulgaria, certain that the Allies would not force Turkey out of the war and convinced that the Central Powers would win it, invaded hard-pressed Serbia. Within a month Serbia was overrun by Austrian, German, and Bulgarian troops. This allowed the Austrians, with a huge and well-equipped though remarkably old-fashioned army, to concentrate against the Russians and Italians, who had entered the war on May 23, 1915. More immediately important, with Serbia in Austrian hands and Bulgaria now one of the Central Powers, Germany was connected with Turkey by railway. The Turkish Army now could be equipped and supplied. The eastern Mediterranean and much of the Near East was now closed to the Allies, and Russia remained isolated.

Finally, of overriding significance, the failure against Turkey closed the possibilities for battle on the Central Powers' southern flank. The war would have to be won or lost in a head-on attack upon Germany in France and Belgium. For better or worse, after 1915 the Western Front was the only theater that counted.

THE DECLINE OF ASQUITH

The Gallipoli expedition exercised British politics like no other operation of the war, some of which were far larger. Its failure reflected upon the competence and above all the judgment of the First Lord of the Admiralty, Winston Churchill. But more significantly it focused political attention on questions that had been circulating for many months about whether Prime Minister H. H. Asquith, unquestionably a man of experience, probity, and courage, possessed the necessary zeal to head the British government during a desperate war.

There was a curious duality about Asquith's personality that has remained a conundrum for historians. Each of his undeniable strengths was attended by a corresponding weakness. His singular, Aristotelian, clarity of thought, which in the House of Commons earned him the nickname of "the Hammer" for his efficiency in exploiting a fault in an opponent's logic, was undone by the inability to assess with any detachment his own political position in a crisis. It was this unwarranted conviction of his own invulnerability that finally cost him the Prime Ministership in December 1916. For a man trained as a barrister, for three decades a Member of Parliament (MP) and Prime Minister since 1908, he retained a remarkable dislike of conflict. He loved office, it was said, but hated politics. Asquith hated disputes in Cabinet and would adjourn a meeting to avoid one. Skillful ministers such as his successor, David Lloyd George, took advantage of this love of peace and quiet by provoking a row in order to forestall or sometimes to hasten a decision.

Asquith's problem as a war leader proceeded from precisely the characteristics that had made his government between 1908 and 1914 conspicuously successful and productive. He was less a leader than a counselor. His position within the Cabinet, observed Lloyd George, was that of a senior, immensely experienced, but detached, advisor. In Cabinet he was a judge, not an advocate. He would support a program, proposed by someone else, and when asked for legal or political advice, his judgment was admirable. He was fully informed, but never a part of the process. He never said, "This is what we must do." He was far more concerned with avoiding unpleasantness in Cabinet and arriving at an agreed conclusion to a problem than in driving the Cabinet toward any particular goal of his own.

Before the war, with a talented and enthusiastic Cabinet exploding with ideas, Asquith's posture as a disinterested, expert, observer worked well enough. His government to 1914 was one of the most productive of the twentieth century. But his Olympian detachment—a phrase frequently used to describe Asquith—was disastrous in war.

Asquith understood well enough what would work in ordinary politics. He had no knowledge of, nor indeed interest in, military affairs. The military departments, that is Herbert, Lord Kitchener, at the War Office and Winston Churchill at the Admiralty, neither gave Asquith and his Cabinet information nor sought their advice. Hence strategic political direction did not exist. The murderous Dardanelles-Gallipoli operation of 1915, a perfectly respectable military undertaking, collapsed because of a lack of central political control that Asquith should have provided. He allowed Churchill to proceed with a naval and later military operation that was sound in theory only. Ultimately it destroyed Asquith's own Liberal government and might, except for Lloyd George's courage in bringing him back, have banished Churchill from politics.

Asquith's replacement by Lloyd George in December 1916 was not the result of a political conspiracy. Rather it was the product of the gradual erosion of the Prime Minister's position caused largely by himself, by his invariable good humor, his comfortable addiction to good food and drink and evenings of bridge, and his absolute refusal either to forbid or to order action. In the end there were too many men who, even in their admiration for Asquith, knew that under his leadership Britain would lose the war, and who felt uncomfortably that the man to win it was David Lloyd George.

Asquith's decline and fall occupied eighteen months and occurred in two steps. The crisis of his government that began on May 15, 1915, was not entirely the result of Gallipoli. Indeed, it was not clear at that time, nor is it today, that the military leadership did not deserve more of the blame for the disaster. But it was the government that came under fire. At least since the beginning of 1915 there had been grumbling in the press and among politicians about government, referring to Asquith's "slackness" and "lethargy." Cabinet members, notably Churchill, it was said, were out of control. There seemed to be no planning for war. Hard decisions on the mobilization of industry were not taken in a timely fashion or at all. Above all there were rumors about devastating shortages of equipment and ammunition at the front. It must be quickly noted that these criticisms came from members of both parties and in a greater or lesser degree from all newspapers. This was clearly not partisan bickering but a generalized, nervous discontent centering upon the Prime Minister. Official assurances, many from Asquith himself, that the B.E.F. was better cared for, better fed, and better trained than any British army in history—all perfectly true—did nothing to allay them. Nor did the official false claims that the Germans were growing weaker by the day provide reassurance.

Hence there already existed a reservoir of unhappiness ready to overflow when on Saturday, May 15, 1915, the First Sea Lord at the Board of Admiralty, Admiral John, Lord Fisher, resigned. He had done so, he announced, because of his opposition to the Dardanelles-Gallipoli operation. Fisher's resignation may be counted as the occasion, but not the cause, of the collapse of the Liberal government which had ruled Britain with splendid success and amid great controversy since December of 1905. Within forty-eight hours the leaders of both parties had agreed that there would have to be an all-party Cabinet. The Prime Minister did not argue. Both he and the leader of the Conservatives, Andrew Bonar Law, were under heavy pressure from their own followers, Asquith for failure to manage his government, Bonar Law for feebleness in attacking him on its failures. Each man would be strengthened, and safer, if he worked with the other.

Asquith and Bonar Law agreed upon a coalition on Monday, May 17, and the new coalition government, with Asquith remaining Prime Minister, was announced on May 25. There were some remarkable changes. Churchill, of course, had to leave the Admiralty, to be replaced by a Conservative. For the time being, he remained politically active only in a minor post at the fringes of the ministry. A Labour Member of Parliament, Arthur Henderson, took the Board of Education, becoming the first member of his party to serve in any Cabinet post. However, the sensational innovation in the new Cabinet was the appearance of an entirely new department of government, the Ministry of Munitions, to be headed by the former Chancellor of the Exchequer, David Lloyd George.

The Ministry of Munitions represented, first of all, a massive attempt by a desperate government to organize Britain's vast manufacturing resources to meet the demands of the escalating war upon which the nation had embarked so casually eleven months earlier. In this regard, the new ministry was unquestionably a great success. It manufactured directly and through private contractors, weapons and ammunition in an ever-increasing torrent. It also conducted research, designed, developed, and tested new weapons from the modern fragmentation grenade to the battle tank to the SE5 airplane. By the end of the war it was employing, both directly and indirectly, hundreds of thousands of men and, significantly, women, at decent wages while providing around many of the new factories model living accommodations, canteens, and recreation facilities. Secondly, the Ministry of Munitions was quickly perceived as a gigantic and successful experiment in democratic collectivized industry. If the government could do these things in war, it would soon be asked, why not in peace? If it could manufacture efficiently and quickly the machines for killing should it not turn its hand to machines for living? Munitions' success during the war provided a telling argument for state intervention in reconstruction after the conflict. It offered a model, to be cited repeatedly for years. Nationalization of industry became and is likely to remain a central doctrine in the economic program of the British Labour party.

CONSCRIPTION, THE SOMME, THE FALL OF ASQUITH AND LIBERALISM, 1916

The coalition government of May 1915 did not work well. Decisionmaking slowed; war planning became more, not less, difficult. Bonar Law, under the spell of Asquith's powerful presence, remained hesitant to demand action. Newspaper criticism of the government quickly revived although the Prime Minister himself tended to be spared by Liberal papers. However, the issue that sapped the strength of the 1915–16 coalition and inaugurated the second phase of Asquith's decline, dividing both Liberal and Conservative members of the Cabinet not only against each other but against their party supporters, was the clear need by the autumn of 1915, for military conscription.

The underlying cause of the fall of the Asquith coalition in the first week of December 1916 proceeded from the Prime Minister's reluctance and indecision in mobilizing his party to deal with the army's need for manpower. Ironically, only months after the formation of the first coalition, Conservative disaffection revived over compulsory military service. By the end of 1915 there existed an organized group of Conservative MPs under the leadership of the sinister and ruthless Sir Edward Carson which for practical purposes repudiated the leadership of the party's nominal head, Bonar Law. It was Carson's Unionist War Committee, super patriots dedicated to the defeat of Germany without compromise, who would pull Asquith down.

The Prime Minister put off consideration of a military draft as long as he could. Supporting him, in effect the opposition to the victory-at-all-costs Unionist War Committee, was a sizable body of more radical Liberals including all the Liberal Cabinet members, except Lloyd George, and most of the more radical Liberal newspapers. These groups must be delineated carefully. Along the fault lines opened by the conscription debate, the Liberal party eventually split and collapsed, making Asquith a martyr. The anticonscriptionists believed, quite accurately, that they represented the conscience of Liberalism, which stood for the right of the individual to choose his political representatives, his vocation, his form of government, and whether he should serve in the army. Liberal editors often went a good deal further than this, asserting, for example, that the government intended eventually to conscript labor. But generally, for a great many highly principled politicians and journalists, military conscription represented the negation of everything their party stood for. In many cases the same people had opposed Britain's entry into the war and had been converted only by the German invasion of Belgium. All were certain that conscription represented a devil's liaison between the Conservative warhawks in Parliament, the Conservative press, and David Lloyd George, who was aiming to unseat their revered Prime Minister.

With his customary political dexterity, Asquith eventually allowed himself to be forced by the clear statistics of declining enlistment coupled with the existence of a large pool of economically unessential, but physically fit, men to bring forward a bill in January 1916 requiring unmarried men to join the army. This, the so-called Bachelor's Bill, was a political subterfuge. It would not bring in many men. Its goal simply was to establish the principle of conscription without offending too greatly Asquith's loyal following among the radical Liberals. As was his custom, Asquith tried to buy time.

He bought very little. Within weeks it was clear that the compulsory enlistment of unmarried men produced only a few more men than had come forward before, while voluntary enlistments now dried up immediately. By March 1916 the Chief of the Imperial General Staff, General Sir William Robertson, was demanding loudly before politicians and in the press that unqualified, general, military conscription be enacted in Britain. Carson threatened a motion of no confidence to bring down the government. Asquith attempted, as he had done in January, to offer the House of Commons a weak compromise measure, essentially an amendment to the Bachelor's Bill. This was contemptuously shouted down by Carson's Unionist War Committee on April 27. The end of the debate came immediately. As probably he had intended to do, Asquith surrendered after making a show of resistance. Early in May he introduced a universal Military Service Bill. It became law on May 25, 1916.

Asquith, and classical Liberalism, now had been mortally wounded. For nine months the Prime Minister, with the support of the great majority of the senior members of his party both in and out of the government, had dithered and hesitated about a measure that eventually would have to be approved. And more damaging appeared the larger issue outside of the question of compulsory military service: could men with such principles, admirable as they were for peacetime administration, successfully make the hard decisions that would be necessary to prosecute a desperate war? Many MPs, and many voters, determined after the conscription debates that they could not. Attention turned to the man who many believed could win the war if it were still winnable, the man who had resolved the munitions crisis, the "man of push and go" who had "delivered the goods": David Lloyd George.

The year 1916 was a turning point in established British political practice. The balance of political force tipped away from the old governing class to the new order of populist, sometimes demagogic, democracy. What Crane Brinton referred to as the Victorian Compromise, the unspoken agreement between the ancient political parties to seek change of government but not change of principle, now disappeared. This new reckless temper had certainly appeared before the war. David Lloyd George himself was a part of it. It became permanent in 1916.

After conscription was enacted Britain's first experience with mass slaughter followed quickly. Indeed in the spring the Secretary of the War Committee of the Cabinet, Lt. Col. Maurice Hankey, had confided bitterly to his diary that were the army not planning a grand climactic battle, "an orgy of killing," for the summer, conscription would have been unnecessary. But now the army needed an assured supply of heroes. The great attack began on July 1, 1916, when, after an eight-day bombardment of the German lines just to the north of the Somme River, nineteen British divisions moved forward on a front of eighteen miles. In the first six hours of the battle, the British suffered 59,000 casualties of whom 19,000 were killed. By the time the attack wound down in mid-November British casualties amounted to 419,000, nearly two-thirds of the number of casualties suffered by the army, navy, and air force together in the entire six years of the Second World War. The deepest penetration at the front had been six miles of tortured ground (later all lost, with much more, in March 1918).

To say that the Battle of the Somme was traumatic is to dilute the reality of a national horror by modern jargon. The losses could not be concealed. Anyone could read the eight-column lists of officer casualties in *The Times*, or visit the streets full of ambulances lined up before Waterloo station to carry away the daily consignment of wounded, the "butcher's bill." In this way, within the first few weeks, between July and September 1916, the war came home to Britain. The conflict in France had certainly caused casualties before, indeed in the tens of thousands as at Loos in September 1915, but these largely had been regular troops and reservists whose numbers could be hidden by censorship. Now the dead and wounded numbering in the hundreds of thousands were well over half volunteers. Tragically, the British system of recruiting on a territorial (county) or on an affinity basis (common interest or place of work, the so-called "pals" battalions), meant that an entire country village or city neighborhood (East Belfast of the 36th [Ulster] Division for example) might suddenly learn that most of their young men were dead or wounded or, most terrifying of all, missing. The fatal telegram: "The Secretary of State regrets to inform you . . . ," followed some days later by an awkward, mechanical, yet anguished, letter from the company commander, all became and would remain the shared misery and remembrance of the Great War.

The impact of the Somme battle on the popular consciousness was complex but clear. By the time the battle ended in mid-November the public reaction was less of pacifism than despair. If the war could not be won by the sacrifice of nearly half a million trained and fully equipped young men, how could it be won at all? Inevitably, fingers began to point at British leadership, both political and military. Generals in splendid uniforms were held up as either incompetent timeservers or bloodthirsty, glory-seeking, uncaring, savages. The politicians who were supposed to control them were concerned with nothing but party and office. This boiled down to a generalized sense that under the present administration the war could not be won. To deduce the public temper of the time in the absence of public opinion polls may be foolhardy; nevertheless, in the late autumn of 1916 there is more evidence than usual to support the contention of popular disillusion with the Asquith government. Asquith himself believed that if there were an election at the end of 1916, forced perhaps by the House of Lords, his party would be heavily defeated. It has not been noted by historians of the war—although political leaders at the time never forgot it—that the House of

Lords, almost totally Conservative, proconscription and prowar, could cause an election at any time by refusing to agree to the postponement of the overdue general election required under the Parliament Act of 1911. The winner in such a contest would be Carson's Unionist War Committee.

When the final crisis arrived, in the beginning of December 1916, the replacement of Herbert Asquith as Prime Minister by David Lloyd George was less the result of conspiracy than of Asquith's own stubbornness or arrogance. Lloyd George and Edward Carson, with the reluctant support of Bonar Law, proposed the creation of a small committee, not larger than three or four men, subsidiary to the Cabinet, which would devote itself exclusively to the political direction of the war. The Prime Minister, pointedly, would not be a member. Asquith did not like the plan, but at first, on December 3, seems to have accepted it. Then, at the urging of the other Liberal members of the Cabinet, most of whom detested Lloyd George and doubted his loyalty to the Prime Minister, Asquith changed his mind and refused to countenance any War Council of which he was not a part, whereupon Lloyd George resigned from the government.

In the public mind, and in Conservative newspapers, Lloyd George was unquestionably the most visible and successful member of the Asquith administration. Many people assumed Lloyd George intended to replace Asquith, although Lloyd George insisted to anyone who would listen that the small war directorate was not a plot to overthrow Asquith. Asquith's presence at the head of the government was indispensable, said Lloyd George. For the moment this was probably true. But the intensely loyal Liberal ministers by whom the Prime Minister was surrounded convinced him otherwise. The proper response in constitutional terms, they argued on December 4, should be Asquith's own resignation. The contest between the two men should be referred to the will of the House of Commons. They reasoned that Lloyd George would not be able to form a government, with the total devotion of the Liberal MPs to Asquith. Only Asquith, they argued, could command the House of Commons. Constitutionally this advice was proper, but the effect was to transform an adjudicable discussion of how best to manage the British war effort into a public contest between Lloyd George and the Prime Minister. More narrowly, Asquith, with the greatest confidence, had allowed his own person to become the focus of the dispute. The next day, December 5, 1916, Asquith resigned on behalf of the government. In fact, he had already asked, two days before, for the resignation of the members of the Cabinet.

This was a fatal mistake. Despite the assurances of the Liberal ministers that Lloyd George had no support except a few score Conservative hotheads and that Asquith inevitably would be invited back, within two days Lloyd George had put together a ministry supported by all of the Conservatives in the House of Commons and, to Asquith's dismay, by a substantial majority of the Liberals as well as by the Labour party. The names of the new administration appeared in the newspapers on December 10, 1916.

Asquith must be listed as a casualty of the Great War as surely as was his adored son Raymond, who fell at the Somme only a few weeks earlier. With Asquith died the great Liberal party of Palmerston and Gladstone and the tradition of civility and humanity in politics. These traditions began to fade in the last decade before the war. The rising violence in partisan behavior, the violent protest by suffragettes, the Irish, the trade union radicals, and indeed the ferocity of the attacks on the House of Lords by Lloyd George himself provide the evidence. Certainly these facts are true and the illiberal, uncivil behavior of the partisans of the new politics was denounced roundly by contemporaries as being ungentlemanly and un-English. Lloyd George himself would have retorted, as indeed he did on a few occasions, that he was neither a gentleman nor an Englishman. He was only a Welsh country solicitor who was trying to win a war.

Still, the palpable fact was that the style of administration and, of greater importance, the decency and the approach to government that Asquith and his Liberal advisors represented, were unsuited to winning the war. Nor were they adapted to the class-based corporate politics that followed it. The war demanded the compulsory organization of industry, labor, and citizen manpower. Gladstonian Liberalism held that a British citizen, if he were content only to collect dividend checks, or in other cases to go hungry, should be allowed to do nothing if he wished; the overarching duty of government was the protection of individual liberty. The only determinant of behavior was an individual's sense of obligation to the community, always modified to be sure, by economic advantage. In the long run, these excellent doctrines would redound to the betterment of all, and so they generally had done throughout the nineteenth century.

Thus the war provided the occasion for the demise both of the Liberal party and of the old tradition of liberal politics it expounded. The end came quickly. After the general election of 1918 the Labour party with its foundations of socialist doctrine, trade unionism, and class-based organization succeeded the Liberal party as the official opposition. The government benches opposite, Stanley Baldwin is said to have commented, resembled a convention "of hard faced businessmen who looked as if they had done well out of the war." A different sort of politics appeared during the war as well as a different sort of politician, of whom David Lloyd George, who indeed had done well out of the war, was an early example.

3 / THE PEACE,
POSTWAR BRITAIN

THE CRISIS OF 1917–1918

The winter of 1916–17 marked the beginning of the third phase of the Great War, a fact recognized in all the belligerent countries. The massive attacks of the previous spring and summer, the Battles of Verdun and of the Somme and the great Brusilov offensive in Russia, showed that even the maximum effort of which the attacking armies were capable had moved them no closer to victory. As in Britain, there arose demands in each nation for new ideas, new faces, more daring plans, or for a compromise peace. Torn by civil strife, the Czar's government in Russia collapsed. The new Emperor of Austria clumsily began secret negotiations to take his nation out of the war lest he suffer a similar fate. The venerable commander of the French armies, the hero of the Marne, General Joseph Joffre, held responsible for 1,000,000 French battlefield deaths since the beginning of the war and the failure to prepare for the German attack at Verdun, was summarily replaced by General Robert Georges Nivelle. A month later, on January 31, 1917, Germany announced the commencement of unrestricted submarine warfare in the full knowledge that this act would bring the United States into the war. The United States did finally declare war on April 6, 1917; by that time German submarines were sinking one vessel out of every four that entered or left British ports. At that rate, Britain would be on the verge of starvation within a few weeks.

In the same dreadful month, on April 16, 1917, the new French commander, General Nivelle, began a long-planned major offensive in Champagne. By attacking on a very narrow front with only a short artillery preparation but with a large force, Nivelle assured the British government he would not merely push back, but would break through the German lines and restore the war of movement. Instead the French were repulsed with huge losses and in the middle of May began a widespread refusal of orders within units of the French army. These were not really mutinies, although they were so termed. Rather, they were more in the nature of military strikes. Nonetheless, by the first week of June 1917, French military forces were almost paralyzed. The French did not fully recover for nearly a year. Meanwhile the Russian war effort wasted away while the United States appeared to be unable to organize itself for war, and the German submarine remained unconquered. The devastating result was that Britain, possessing the only Allied army that was both in the field and under discipline, fought alone from the summer of 1917 to the spring of 1918 as it would do for a similar period in 1940 and 1941. The sinister alternatives, win or die, were not as pikestaff clear as in 1940, but it remains a noble hour.

Though the fighting was valiant, it does not follow that British military power was well handled. Between July and November 1917 the British generals wasted what was probably the best force the nation had ever possessed—trained, fully equipped, and experienced—in a futile attack in Belgium. This operation, known variously as the Flanders offensive, the third Ypres, or the Passchendaele offensive, cost 300,000 casualties, not many fewer than on the Somme. By the time the Flanders offensive ended, the Bolshevik revolution had occurred in Russia, and Russian army resistance, which had been slowing for six months, ceased altogether. For their part the Germans, fully aware of the diminishing threat in the East, had begun months earlier the systematic transfer of divisions to the Western Front. By Christmas British intelligence could identify nearly two hundred enemy divisions in northeast France and Belgium. For the first time since 1914 the Germans outnumbered the Allies in the West. They would surely attack before the Americans came. The French remained passive. Could Britain hold them alone or would the war, after three years of sacrifice, be finally lost?

The expected German attack, on the old Somme battlefield, began on March 21, 1918 in great force, using new assault tactics. Within five days the Germans had advanced thirty miles, the deepest penetration in the West since 1914, threatening the railroad center of Amiens. That city's fall would have cut off supplies from the British armies in the North requiring a retreat that would uncover the Channel ports. The crisis before Amiens finally stirred the French army. Reinforcements were rushed to the city. To provide an extra incentive for this revival of French activity, the Allies, including the United States and Italy, agreed that the French general Ferdinand Foch be appointed supreme commander with the responsibility for all forces in France. In the end Amiens was held.

The attack of March 21 was the first of four great German offensives between March and July of 1918. The last, before Paris against the French and now the United States army, was contained on July 17. General Foch ordered an immediate Allied attack on all fronts, which the French and Americans undertook the next day and the British on August 8. The Germans began a general retreat that continued until their surrender on November 11, 1918.

THE NEW PRIME MINISTER, THE GENERAL ELECTION

The coalition government that came into being at the beginning of December 1916 represented so great a departure from the century-old traditions of English parliamentarianism that it fully deserved the epithet often applied to it at the time, "revolutionary." The customary usages of Cabinet solidarity and collective decisionmaking disappeared. Essentially, Britain was governed by a one-man presidential administration conducted by David Lloyd George.

The man himself, the exemplar and advocate of the new politics, deserves a moment's attention. When he entered the House of Commons in 1890 at twenty-seven, he had been an outsider, poor, worst of all Welsh, a "different, a cheaper sort of M.P." explained one of them. "Taffy was a Welshman and Taffy was a thief" went an English nursery epigram. He had therefore to fight not only the battle for attention, demanded of all new Members of Parliament, but for equality in the tangled thicket of English social snobbery. He won the first battle with appointment to Henry Campbell-Bannerman's Cabinet in 1905. He had learned quickly that although the House of Commons might laugh at him in the Members' Smoking Room it responded quickly to the voters' discontent raised by his speeches of matchless eloquence made on the outside. At the end of July 1909 he had forced the House of Lords, by insulting them into a fury, to veto his 1909 budget, so beginning the chain of events that brought the Parliament Act of 1911 and the sinister Home Rule crisis of 1914.

Despite his political successes, Lloyd George could never conquer the perception of which he was fully aware, that he did not "belong." Even as he became Prime Minister he was the charlatan genius, the flawed leader. Men admired him for his courage, his quick perception of problems, his industry, his charm, even as they deplored or despised his Welsh mendacity, his common tastes. Many in December 1916 who supported and admired him, hated themselves for doing so.

In the end after a political life covering fifty-five years, he remained one of those men—there are many—who are admired but not loved. The good fairies gave him every quality for leadership, but the bad fairy had decreed: "Men will not trust him."

Lloyd George as prime minister assembled around himself a small group of four, later five, men that, although designated a "War Cabinet," was in no sense equal with the Prime Minister first among them that British constitutionalists were accustomed to seeing. The executive authority of the War Cabinet lay in the hands of Lloyd George alone. The other men, with the exception of Andrew Bonar Law, who was Chancellor of the Exchequer and Conservative leader, had no departmental responsibilities. They were in no sense nonentities, but saving Bonar Law, their appointments derived from administrative ability not political leverage. One of them, Jan Christian Smuts of South Africa, had not even a seat in Parliament and declined to seek one. The members of the War Cabinet, again with the exception of Bonar Law, carried out varied tasks as assigned by the Prime Minister. They were efficient, specialist technicians who provided expert advice on matters in which the Prime Minster felt he needed it.

Jan Christian Smuts, for example, effectively created the Royal Air Force in early 1918, when charged with finding a means of defense of British cities against German bombing. The Royal Flying Corps, preoccupied with military operations in France, could not or did not provide protection for British cities. Smuts proposed an independent department of government, a ministry for air, with statutory responsibility for air cover of the army and navy and as well the air defense of Britain. (Looking ahead to the Second World War, this essentially political solution to a military problem, although it included the administrative framework for the magnificent Fighter Command that saved Britain in the summer of 1940, at the same time destroyed the Royal Naval Air Service, so putting the Royal Navy a generation behind Japan and the United States in aviation.)

Under the new War Cabinet were the old Departments of State, whose ministers now were no longer members of the Cabinet and who accordingly were not involved in the making of war policy. Nor, it should be noted, were these ministers responsible to Parliament for government decisions beyond the conduct of their own ministries. As the War Cabinet finally evolved, some departmental ministers, the War and Foreign Offices and the Admiralty, were regularly invited to its nearly daily meetings as were any number of service officers and the Directors General of Military and Naval Intelligence. The War Cabinet was never, therefore, the private, intimate, central brain of British power that Lloyd George had envisioned. But emphatically it possessed what the old Cabinet always lacked, a larger, indeed perhaps too large, fund of up-to-date, often raw, information upon which it could make instant determinations. It is not clear that the British government's decisions under Lloyd George were better, more clever, or more farseeing, than its decisions under Asquith, but there can be no doubt that they resulted in action more quickly and with more immediate effect. The decisions belonged to one man.

As this essay attempts to indicate in advance those evolutions in twentieth century British history that subsequently became significant, the presidential War Cabinet, deserves a few remarks. Churchill revived the system in the second war when he became Prime Minister on May 10, 1940, without however insisting upon the clear division between departmental management and war planning detachment. Churchill created for himself the new office of Minister of Defence. More important—perhaps to be accounted for by Churchill's imperious nature—the War Cabinet personnel tended to be cronies, or sometimes errand boys, rather than senior politicians of proven ability: Lord Beaverbrook, Lord Cherwell, John Anderson (a civil servant), Oliver Lyttelton, or Brendan Bracken. These were men whom Churchill, for his own reasons, wished to keep around him, moving them from office to office within his entourage. Some were certainly extremely clever, but with a few exceptions they were hardly seasoned ministers of the Crown. Churchill's War Cabinet was more a royal court than an administrative brain.

When Lloyd George replaced Herbert Asquith as Prime Minister there existed a widespread assumption among Liberals, infecting possibly not a few Conservatives, that his government could not last long. No senior Liberals supported him. Asquith remained leader of the Liberals and commanded the loyalty of all the senior party members. Lloyd George, it was assumed, was a prisoner of the Conservatives who would use him and discard him.

Lloyd George was able to demonstrate that these assumptions were mistaken in the only serious attempt by the Liberals to unseat him, the so-called "Maurice Debate" on May 9, 1918, over a lie he supposedly told the House of Commons. The vote at that time showed that Asquith controlled fewer than half the Liberals in the House of Commons. Nonetheless, Lloyd George was Prime Minster without an organized party. Asquith controlled the party machinery, party funds, and dominated most constituency associations.

These facts troubled Lloyd George greatly. There had been no general election since December 1910. Asquith in 1916 had summoned a committee under the Speaker of the House of Commons to consider reform of the electoral laws. It reported soon after Lloyd George's accession. From this came in 1918 a complete overhaul of the franchise, the Fourth Reform Act, granting the vote to all male citizens over age twenty-one and to all women over thirty without restriction of residence. The electorate was thus tripled in size. In the summer of 1918 the Allied governments uniformly assumed that the war would last well into 1919 and would require an invasion of Germany. But with a new law on the books and an eight-year-old House of Commons, chosen before the war over issues no longer of any concern, an election could not be postponed again. Moreover, the Prime Minister hoped that a wartime election would make possible the diversion of questions on the treatment of defeated Germany. It would always be possible to say that such matters should wait upon victory. Instead, he intended, the government's theme would be the reconstruction of Britain, "a land fit for heroes to live in." And so, even without a party, he would call an election.

Lloyd George made the preliminary decision in August 1918. His difficulty was that without a party, except for the 140 to 150 Liberal MPs who supported him in the House of Commons, he would need the services of the Conservative party organization for a campaign in the 707 constituencies created by the 1918 reform act. (Thirty-seven new seats were added to the House of Commons to reduce Ireland's massive overrepresentation. England received thirty-five, Scotland and Wales one each.) In the election the Lloyd George Liberals and the Conservatives would present themselves to the voters as a single political unit. The two parties of the coalition would refrain from contesting seats against each other. Accordingly, September and October saw delicate negotiations between the two parties of the coalition over the allocation of constituencies between Liberal and Conservative candidates. Because Lloyd George was determined that no Liberal supporter of himself should contest a seat for which a supporter of Asquith was also a candidate, the coalition Liberals had to allow Conservatives to stand for nearly all traditionally Liberal seats. Here lay the reason for the quick electoral demise of the Liberal party. Once lost these seats were never regained.

These careful plans for what Lloyd George and Bonar Law expected to be an uneventful wartime election in which every controversial issue could be postponed on the plea of national unity necessary for victory, suddenly became obsolete with Germany's surrender. At the end of October came reports that revolution had broken out in Germany. This news was quickly followed at the beginning of November by a German request for an armistice. So the wartime election became a victory election. "Peace stole upon us like a thief in the night," grumbled

Winston Churchill whom the Prime Minister, at much cost to his own popularity among the Conservatives, had brought back into the government at the Ministry of Munitions in July 1917. The treatment of Germany, not grand promises of reconstruction, would now be the issue.

The two party leaders announced early in November that the election would take place on December 14, 1918. The sudden surrender of Germany on November 11 probably increased the certainty of a coalition victory in the election. But it altered its character entirely. Military victory trivialized the political campaign. Instead of being a celebration of national determination, the election became a contest among individual candidates to prove their hatred for the defeated Central Powers. The only domestic topic was an expression of some contempt for Lloyd George for his unseemly appropriation of the heroism of British soldiers to ensure himself continued residence at No. 10 Downing Street. Because of the large number of parties involved in the election, many with the same name, each leader of the coalition parties sent an open letter to each candidate of his party naming him or her as the party's official choice and asking for loyal voters' support (sixteen women ran, for the first time; one was elected in Ireland but did not take her seat). This message was styled a "coupon," a term first used derisively by Asquith. It provided the customary historical soubriquet for the election of 1918, the "Coupon Election."

The general election campaign of November and December 1918 occurred in a public atmosphere dominated and indeed disfigured by the hysterical euphoria brought by the German surrender. By the end of November this had turned into an equally mindless fury caused by the truly pitiable condition of British prisoners of war who began to return to Britain about two weeks after the Armistice. Someone should be punished, became the cry. This evolved within a few days into the demand that all Germany should be punished and the Kaiser kidnapped from Holland to which he had fled on November 9, brought to England, given, of course, a fair trial, and then hanged.

The violence of the public mood, orchestrated by many newspapers, inevitably affected the 1,625 parliamentary candidates. Instead of presenting a list of vague promises about a better Britain after the war, the slogan of coalition candidates became "make Germany pay." In the minds of many voters the two goals were connected: somehow Germany would finance British reconstruction. Emphatically this was not the election that Lloyd George and Bonar Law had intended to fight. A new Britain, not a devastated Germany, had been planned as the theme. To their credit, despite heavy pressure from the press, both men resisted demands for an attack upon Germany until the last few days before the poll.

The outcome of the voting in December 1918 was never really in doubt. When the results were announced on December 28 (delayed to permit a tally of the soldiers' vote) the coalition had won overwhelmingly. Perhaps most significant, or tragic for British politics, was the almost total destruction of the Asquithian Liberals who returned only twenty-eight. Asquith himself lost the seat he had held for thirty-two years to an unknown independent candidate. Labour's performance was not markedly better, even though it had fought the election for the first time as a national, rather than a regional, party. Nonetheless, with sixty-three Members, it emerged as the largest opposition group. It was not immediately apparent, but Liberalism had disappeared in a wave of voter madness.

The 1918 general election proved an indicator of the transformation of British politics and society since 1914. In 1914 the Liberals had been the governing party for nine years. They were in deep trouble over Ireland to be sure, but they had behind them a brilliant record of legislative accomplishment and were solidly united behind their leader Herbert Asquith. They might well have lost the next election due by the end of 1915, but no one questioned their place as one of the two great parties of government. By the end of 1918 they were gone, banished to the fringes of British politics, never again to control a government. Liberalism was not pushed aside, or superseded, by the Labour party. It took nearly a generation, until 1945, for the Labour party to mature enough to form a government without a coalition partner. Liberalism killed itself in the fratricidal battles that began with conscription in 1915. The true inheritors of the Liberal voters, of their parliamentary seats and indeed of much of their program, were the Conservatives. In the twenty-six-and-a-half years between the elections of December 1918 and July 1945 the Conservatives controlled the House of Commons for all but thirty-five months.

THE PROBLEMS OF PEACEMAKING

The election of December 1918 left Prime Minister David Lloyd George a captive of the Conservatives who alone, after the departure of the Sinn Fein party, commanded a majority in the House of Commons. Only the loyalty of the Conservative leaders in the Cabinet, fortified by his own astonishing popularity in the country, kept Lloyd George in power. A good many political observers, Conservative leader Andrew Bonar Law as well as a number of newspaper editors, felt that Lloyd George's popularity alone could have won him the election, even without Conservative support.

The election madness of 1918 had an immediate effect on British diplomacy. At the Paris Peace Conference, which began only weeks after the election, it forced Britain however unwillingly to conspire with France in that nation's attempt to destroy by diplomacy a Germany which had not been invaded, whose industrial machine remained intact and whose people were only demoralized and tired. After the fighting stopped it was clear that the German army, ominously, had not fallen apart as defeated armies do. Article II of the Armistice agreement of November 11 had specified that within fifteen days the German army was to evacuate all Belgian and French territory as well as the former French provinces of Alsace and Lorraine and to surrender vast amounts of military hardware. As the Allied troops advanced immediately following the Germans' withdrawal, they found the abandoned German encampments with tents in precise rows, rifles stacked, helmets placed in neat lines. Everything had been done under orders. This was an army still under discipline. The sparkling professionalism of the German army remained intact and would appear again in 1939.

The French understood all of this perfectly well and fear of German military expertise and economic power would govern French diplomacy throughout the interwar period. From the French point of view, Germany had surrendered prematurely and France could not depend upon the concatenation of events that had brought most of the world to its aid by 1918 to occur again. Germany, still dangerous, would have to be rendered impotent by the peace treaty. After the war France would have to prepare for Germany's inevitable war of revenge. French leaders could also ponder on the fact that during the war their nation's birthrate, already declining in 1914, had fallen precipitously. This would mean fewer young men available for the army in the middle 1930s. In twenty years Germany would be stronger in comparison to France than it had been in 1914.

These factors governed French behavior at the Paris peace conference, its treatment of Germany deriving from its own need for security and economic revival, exacerbated by the desire for revenge. France certainly could worry not about the needs of European stability. The war in the west had devastated some of the richest areas of both France and Belgium, while since 1914 not one Allied soldier with a rifle in his hand had set foot upon German soil. The only constraint, common to all the Allies, was the fear that a Germany completely devastated would turn to Communism.

These barriers of French intransigence and of the December 1918 election confounded British diplomacy at Paris. So far as possible the French were determined to destroy Germany with a punitive treaty while the British coalition government's campaign promises to "make Germany pay" rendered it impossible for Lloyd George to resist. In March 1919, when at the head of the British delegation, Lloyd George began to show signs of softness in the matter of war reparations, he received a telegram signed by over 300 newly elected MPs reminding him that the government was pledged to "make Germany pay." Whether such a policy would destroy it economically could be considered later.

The peace treaty with Germany was signed in a splendid ceremony in the Hall of Mirrors in Louis XIV's palace at Versailles on June 28, 1919, precisely five years after Franz Ferdinand's assassination at Sarajevo. The French piquantly had designated this location because in the same room Chancellor Otto von Bismarck proclaimed the German Empire on January 18, 1871, at the end of the Franco-Prussian war. History, the Germans were to understand, had come full circle.

The treaty deprived Germany of about ten percent of its land area and ten percent of its population, most territories, with their valuable coal and iron ore resources, going to France and Poland. German military and naval forces were severely restricted. Germany could maintain an army no larger than 100,000 men without heavy artillery or aircraft and a navy totalling only 100,000 tons with no single ship larger than 10,000 tons. There could be no submarines of any size.

These stipulations generally had been expected. The return of property seized by Prussia or Germany between 1774 and 1871 and the extinction of militarism, "Prussianism" as it was customarily referred to in Britain, had been stated Allied objectives since the beginning of the war. But the peace treaty carried punitive clauses as well. Article 227 called for the trial by an international court of the "former" German Emperor for "a supreme offense against international morality and the sanctity of treaties." Similar treatment was specified for about 100 other German leaders including army Commander in Chief Paul von Hindenburg whom, in an act that should have been a warning for the future, the German voters elected President of the Republic in 1925. More wounding and humiliating was the requirement that Germany pay a huge, but unstipulated, monetary reparation. This was later set by a commission that in April 1923 found Germany to be liable for the payment by 1963 of $32,000,000,000 in gold, plus interest.

The severe nature of German reparations leaned for their logic upon Article 231 of the treaty in which Germany accepted sole responsibility for all "the loss and damage" caused by the war. The following article, 232, specified accordingly that it would pay for the war's damage and the victorious powers would be permitted by the treaty to enforce the fulfillment of its obligations. Hence the victors possessed the legal right to interfere in German affairs at any time until the debt was paid, observed French Premier George Clemenceau. Within five years after the Armistice, the French would act upon this right. There is much to be said for the theory that so far as the French political and military leadership were concerned the treaty signed at the Versailles palace was less a punishment of Germany for causing the war than for surrendering too soon.

PROFIT AND LOSS FOR BRITAIN

Changes in the Pattern of Life and Employment

In one way or another, the problems raised or left unaddressed by the Versailles treaty would affect, and sometimes dominate, not only British diplomacy but Britain's domestic, political, and worse, economic affairs for the entire interwar period. The coal industry was possibly the worst sufferer. German payments to France in coal destroyed, essentially forever, the British export market in that commodity, the production of which in 1913 had employed a tenth of the nation's male workforce, about 1,000,000 men. British coal production in 1913, 271,000,000 tons, was higher than it had ever been before, or would ever be again. About one-third was exported.

But in 1920, France received far more coal than it required, so the extra supply was simply dumped upon the international market. Between 1920 and 1921 the world price of coal fell by 50 percent. Coal mining became, and would remain, the chronically sick man of British industries. John Maynard Keynes, who had been a member of the British delegation in Paris and had resigned in frustration, pointed out in an angry book published in December 1919, *The Economic Consequences of the Peace*, that despite all the talk of trade rivalry between the two nations, before the war Germany had been Britain's best foreign customer, overtaking the United States in the 1890s. Now Germany was impoverished, in chaos, and liable for ruinous debts that would keep it in that condition, and Britain had connived in its destruction. Whether or not this was good diplomacy, it was economic insanity.

A contributing element to the bitterness of the mining strikes of the 1920s surely arose from the memory of prewar conditions. In the last five years before the war the price of coal and the amount produced had increased almost every year, in line with world inflation. In these years, miners, with a legislated minimum wage in 1912, truly were, as they always had seen themselves, the aristocrats of labor. A miner's household with a father and perhaps two or three sons working in the pit would easily have available the four or five pounds per week that would make it subject to the middle class income tax. Contrary to assertions

made in the interwar period, before 1914 mining families were
not at all impoverished.

When Keynes's book appeared, just six months after the signing of the peace treaty, Britain was still uncomfortably prosperous. The accumulated consumer demand of four-and-one-half
years of wartime scarcity, combined with the savings from high
unspent wages, resulted in a retail purchasing frenzy. Returning soldiers found work easily; wages remained high. There were
shortages of everything from coal to living accommodations to
potatoes. As prices rose there were strikes and threats of strikes
in the coal mines, railway transport, and even among the police.

Keynes's predicted disaster arrived on schedule in the autumn
of 1920. Coal prices fell to one-half of their peak in 1919. The
cost of ocean cargo space on the Baltic Exchange fell similarly.
British shipbuilding and repairing employed, to be sure, many
fewer men than the huge mining workforce, but was immensely
profitable and influential. Before the war British yards generally built half of the world's new tonnage every year, of which
Germany bought a substantial proportion. By 1923, 43 percent
of shipyard workers were unemployed and by 1932, 62 percent.
In 1920 there were yet no accurate statistics for unemployment
but as the cold weather began, the appearance on the streets
of men without work was unmistakable. By Christmas, Britain
had entered the long winter of economic distress from which
it would not emerge for twenty years. A year later, in December 1921 somewhat over 2,000,000 men and women, one-fifth
of the 1913 workforce, were jobless.

Three facts that remained constant until the Second World
War must be emphasized. The first is that after 1925, the economic drought affected principally the old heavy industries,
unhappily those for which Britain had long been famous: shipbuilding, machine tools, textiles, and, above all, coal. As a result, the long depression came to be centered in North England,
Lowland Scotland, Northern Ireland, and Wales. Nearly all the
firms there were export-oriented. Except for coal, the value
added to these products had been the fruit of British technical superiority. And again, with the exception of coal, Germany
and Central Europe to its south had been a critical market.

But second, less depressingly, the 1920s saw in Britain as in the rest of the industrialized world the explosive growth of the vast consumer products industries, many connected with two new sources of power, electricity and the internal combustion engine, each, in a usable form, only about thirty-five years old. The new industries, producing appliances for the home, components for electric apparatus and for the transmission of electricity, automobiles, aircraft, and chemicals, had little in common with the old metal hammering operations of traditional heavy engineering. The new products were fashioned on production lines by semiskilled workers who had learned the assembly-line method during the war. Factories now usually were smaller, better lighted, and cleaner. Women again were present in considerable numbers, hitherto having only been employed in the manufacture of textiles. The new industries tended to be located around the population centers of the West Midlands and in the Southeast, not in the North, which was most important for the effect on British unemployment.

A third trend of the interwar years saw the movement of large numbers of women away from domestic service and into the service industries or government and private employment. The economic suffering proceeding from the unprecedented growth of service industries tended to concentrate in urban areas, especially London. A part of this trend, frequently noted in literature of the 1920s, though not statistically important, was the near disappearance of the great noble houses in London as centers of society. The sale of London mansions, many of which became flats, hotels, or clubs, was a symbol of the decline in the vocation of domestic service among both men and women. The census of 1921, despite its unreliable statistics and clumsy categories, shows a decline of 14 percent or 282,000 from the 1911 census of women employed in "Domestic Offices and Personal Services." This number was in a female population that by 1921 was well over 1,000,000 larger than 1911. (In 1921 about the same number of women and girls were employed in domestic service as in 1881.) Significantly, the number of men in domestic service dropped more slowly, by 8 percent. On the other hand in "Commercial Occupations," such as clerks, typists, and shop assistants, women increased their presence by one-half million, or 360 percent, between 1911 and 1921, and added another 50 percent by 1931. Men in commercial occupations increased in numbers by only 170,000 or 22 percent. It should be remarked that this vast alteration in the character of women's employment was accomplished almost entirely by internal migration within the workforce. Contrary to the usual notion that the war vastly increased the number of women in regular employment, the census figures show that the percentage of the total number of women employed in 1921 over 1911 had in fact dropped slightly and the numbers at work grew by only 286,000, far less than the increase of those in the single category, Commercial Occupations, alone. Very large numbers of women worked temporarily during the war in factories, as chauffeurs, and to some extent in government offices, far more than in private industry, but nearly all temporarily employed had obediently retired soon after the Armistice. Of those who worked, what they clearly did not do in a great many cases was return to their old occupations. Textiles were declining. Nonetheless, despite endless complaints in literature about the impossibility of finding servants, "Personal (indoor domestic) Service," the new census category adopted in 1921, remained the largest employer of women throughout the 1920s, and indeed increased by 15 percent during the decade. There were 1,390,000 women in domestic service in 1921, 1,509,000 in 1931.

Although statistics for domestic service changed only slightly, the effect of the war on women was profound in this area. In the 1920s women were clerks in shops, secretaries in offices, university students, and professionals, especially in the growing field of government service. This had been exceptional four years earlier, but was now routine. The appearance of professional women was confined almost entirely to population centers, mostly in the south. But the changes spread and were permanent.

Contrary to what is often assumed by historians, the total number of women at work did not rise markedly in the decade after the war. Women numbered 41 percent of the male workforce in 1911 and 42 percent in 1931. But the character of their tasks altered vastly. Was the change in women's status a result of their temporary excursions into male occupations during the war, or was it caused by the altered structure of British industry occasioned by the war, of which women simply took advantage? The latter seems to be the answer.

The war reversed a century-and-a-half of migration in Britain from south to north. London and its suburbs, essentially the Metropolitan Police District, grew by three-quarters of a million in the decade of the 1920s, or nearly 20 percent, Birmingham and Coventry by similar percentages. On the other hand, important centers for textiles and shipbuilding, Bolton and Greenock for example, actually declined in population, as did many small localities. Between 1921 and 1931 in Glamorganshire, the heart of Welsh coal mining, the tonnage of coal produced dropped by 40 percent in ten years and employment by a similar percentage, about 100,000 men. At the same time 25,000 people disappeared entirely from the census.

The 1920s and 1930s saw in Britain a vast evolution from the Victorian and Edwardian style of life, occasioned by the loss of wealth during the war. Functions that once were performed in the home, from entertaining to hair dressing, now went to commercial establishments and hotels. Particularly notable was the construction of very large hotels, of which only a few, the Ritz in Piccadilly, and the Russell and the Imperial in Russell Square, had in fact been built in the decade before the war. Restaurants multiplied, patronized by unmarried men and women, and even by women alone, in a way rarely seen before the war.

The war at once constricted, yet in a way dispersed, Britain's wealth. The old fortunes built upon shipbuilding, textiles, and coal royalties were depleted. Country landowning did not produce, but rather consumed, wealth. Income tax and surtax after the war never took less than 40 percent of a bachelor's annual income of £10,000 and usually took more. Before the war income tax had taken 5 percent of the same number of pounds (then far more valuable). The war had reduced the nation's wealth enormously, but incalculably. This occurred more by the deteriorating value of producing resources, factories, shipyards, mines, and trading patterns than by the expropriation of wealth itself, although this was also substantial. A familiar figure in literature was the impoverished landed gentleman, with great house and broad lands, but without the income to maintain them, selling the Gainesborough portraits of his ancestors one by one, usually to Americans.

Another telling example of the change in the British lifestyle is the disappearance in 1921 of the second-class carriage on British railways when the service was made private again after being operated by the government during the war. Second class had begun in the 1840s when working-class passengers had ridden in open wagons. First-class passengers in carriages were unwilling to have their servants travel in the open, hence the demand for a less opulent but clean means of transportation for them. After the war fewer people travelled with servants so second class disappeared. The anomaly of a first and third class, but no second continued to puzzle Americans until well after the Second World War.

As the narrow world of old wealth diminished, Britain became more open; "public" perhaps would be a better word. Fortunes had been made as well as lost during the war and the figure of the "war profiteer," as a pejorative term, often as unjust as it was unkind, became as well known as "decayed aristocrat." Frequently the war profiteer was either a subcontractor to a government factory or a small primary contractor producing weapons, transport equipment, or uniforms. He had been affected by speeches of men such as David Lloyd George, who had urged factory owners to forego old civilian custom and to put their works at the disposal of King and country. Thousands of such factory owners patriotically had done so, giving up their customers in local factories or the export market. In producing a single product, army khaki for example, in unlimited quantities for a generous and undemanding buyer, a small textile manufacturer could become wealthy beyond belief. But he lost also his prewar clientele. After the war the typical response was to retire and close the mill, rather than trying to rebuild a market. This happened repeatedly in the textile industry, which before the war had been the largest exporter by value in the country. During the conflict the Japanese, although technically also belligerent, had taken over many traditional British markets for cheap cotton cloth in Africa, Asia, and indeed in British colonies.

The war both diluted real wealth and transferred large amounts of somewhat less valuable money into new hands. In the process it opened what had been an exclusive society. Without question after 1918, birth, or its appearance, still counted, but now these things could be arranged; in the early twenties there was a notorious traffic in peerages and baronetcies, hereditary knighthoods. Although the purchase of honors was by no means new, after the war it was simply more public and common, and the Prime Minister allowed dignities to be sold to Conservatives without the recommendation of the party whip. Similarly, the democratization of gentility caused a proliferation of "public" (meaning private) schools. All were expensive and many of limited educational value, unless newly well-to-do parents were concerned only with the obliteration of their child's regional accent. Even among public schools, there was dilution. Lest it be overwhelmed, the ancient, distinguished, and select, Headmasters' Conference of public schools (the *Social Register* of schools as it were) ballooned from eighty before the war to over 180 by 1938. A new organization, the Association of Independent School Headmasters came into existence to accommodate the rest.

The foregoing paragraphs record changes in form rather than in kind and in the velocity of social evolution rather than in the appearance of some new discrete process of extinction and resurrection. Of course British aristocracy had always been open to wealth. And the reckless, impoverished aristocrat who supported himself in unfashionable or criminal ways can easily be found in the eighteenth century. Similarly, the decline of British industrial competitiveness had been a subject of public debate at least since the turn of the century. The emancipation of women coupled with the weakening of Victorian social convention had begun at least by the 1890s. One should recall the symbolic doors that appear in Ibsen's *Doll's House*, Shaw's *Pygmalion*, and repeatedly in Wells's *Anne Veronica*. They were now opening. But the "modern woman," intelligent, handsome and strident, was not new. The tired old aphorisms about changes leaving things the same did not apply after the first war. A new world was being born that was not only different but frightening.

4 / LABOUR AND IRELAND,
PROBLEMS OF THE COALITION

TRADE UNIONS AND POLITICS

During the First World War trade unions became a viable political force in Britain. Although the Labour party had been born two decades earlier, Labour representation in the House of Commons, except in coal mining constituencies, depended upon the forbearance of the Liberal party, the so-called "Gladstone agreement." As one Labour leader, Philip Snowden, admitted in his autobiography, few of his colleagues nor he himself would have survived the elections of 1910 had Liberals contested their seats.

Between 1914 and 1918 trade unions doubled in size, from about 4,000,000 in 1914 to about 8,000,000 in 1921 within a labor force that grew by only 1,000,000 in the same period. Hence, membership in unions in 1921 was 45 percent of the workforce, grown from 18 percent in 1914, and far more in heavy engineering and mining, the core of Britain's older industries. Only in textiles and clothing, which together employed 1,700,000, nearly half the female workforce, did union membership lag. More impressive and more important for this study, the number of union members represented in the Trades Union Congress (TUC), a constituent organization of the Labour party, grew from 2,232,000 in 1913 to 6,500,000 in 1920. There were more card-carrying trade unionists in 1920 than there had been eligible electors under the prewar franchise. Organized labor possessed enormous potential for political and economic power. The obvious question was whether working men and women would vote as a bloc of union members.

The election of 1918 seemed to suggest that a great many did not do so. Despite a major effort to field candidates on a national basis (altogether Labour put forward 388 among 707

52

constituencies) and with a new party constitution that called for the organization of Labour branches in every constituency, Labour candidates were the choice of less than one-third of their potential electorate. Still, with sixty-six Members of Parliament Labour outnumbered the pathetic remnant of Asquithian "free" Liberals—derisively called the "Wee Frees" by the Conservative press. Thus Labour could announce itself as the authentic parliamentary opposition.

The sinister prospect of Labour as the alternative government held the unstable Lloyd George coalition together for nearly four years after the war. No one knew what Labour in power would do, but Tory (Conservative) predictions and rumors, not to mention the speeches and writings of some of Labour's less responsible agitators, all suggested an ominous future for Britain's middle class. There would be a tax on wealth as opposed to income, the so-called "capital levy," and even more frightening, the nationalization of land. There was a feeling that Labour seemed always to be ready to allow Russian Bolshevik revolutionaries to enter the country freely; Labour showed unseemly toleration of the horrible events reported from the Soviet Republic.

These attitudes were reinforced within the Cabinet by weekly reports from a domestic surveillance organization, the Directorate of Intelligence established by Lloyd George in the Home Office, which reported directly to the Home Secretary. Among other activities, the Directorate was regularly intercepting and reading letters to and from Labour party MPs. The Directorate's reports had to be hidden when the Labour party came to office.

Labour attracted popular suspicion and fear because of the diversity of its membership, divided between trade unionists and university intellectuals. But the party suffered more because it was unknown, without a record, and assumed to be both disloyal and incompetent. The cumulative effect upon Conservative minds was that a Labour government would mean revolution, perhaps civil war, with the army and police suborned, disarmed, and impotent.

This anxiety gave Prime Minister Lloyd George the leverage he needed to maintain for three-and-one-half years after the war the obedience, if not the loyalty, of the Conservative rank and file. Only he, Lloyd George insisted, stood between settled government and chaos. As it became clear in by-elections that the Coalition was unpopular with voters in both parties, with the Conservatives for spending too much money and with the Liberals for not spending enough, Lloyd George could always reply to complaints with the whisper: "My resignation will not bring my party to power, nor yours, but Labour." Only his personal popularity with the workers, it was to be understood, lay between Britain and revolution. Of course when Labour finally came to power under Ramsay MacDonald in January 1924, nothing much happened during its nine-month tenure. Not only did the government fail to bring revolution, it failed to do anything.

Within reasonable limits, Lloyd George's assessment of his political position was correct. In the three years between March 1919 and March 1922 the Coalition parties had lost eighteen seats and won two. In the same period the Labour party had won fourteen seats from all other parties and lost one. Yet Lloyd George's power to attract cheering crowds never wavered, even as newspapers of both left and right denounced his government as corrupt, faithless, and supine. Whether the intraparty coup at the Carlton Club on October 19, 1922, when the Conservative rank and file by a vote of 185 to 88 rejected their leaders' advice that the party participate in a second Coupon Election, demonstrated a belief that Lloyd George's power was waning or that the Conservatives' hatred of him simply was so great that they no longer cared, cannot be known. In any case he resigned the same day and Conservative leader Andrew Bonar Law became Prime Minister. Both men expected Labour to win the election that Bonar Law immediately ordered, although according to King George V's diary, Lloyd George expected an unsuccessful Labour government. The King, he said, would soon invite him back. It never happened.

IRELAND

A major factor among many others contributing to the Conservative dislike of Lloyd George proceeded from the Prime Minister's anxiety to solve the Irish problem on almost any terms.

With the passage of the Parliament Act of 1911 abolishing the House of Lords' legislative veto, "Home Rule," legislative independence for Ireland, had become a real, as opposed to a theoretical, political issue. Home Rule could now become law. The rebellious Protestant population in Ulster had threatened to bring down the government in July 1914. It remained fully active after the war, as it is today.

Into the contention between Home Rulers, who demanded the restoration of an Irish Parliament, and the Ulster Unionists who rejected any change at all, appeared a new political group, important only after the first war began. This was Sinn Fein (literally "we ourselves," but often expressed as "ourselves alone"). Sinn Fein had no interest in a Dublin Parliament subordinate to Westminster. It aimed at the complete destruction of the so-called "English Connection." Ireland must be totally free and independent, "a nation once again" as its song declared. Sinn Fein was nominally a political party, although it contested no seats until February 1917. However, as its avowed aim was total Irish freedom, its candidates were pledged, if elected, not to take seats at Westminster.

Sinn Fein had no interest in the war with Germany and brought itself first to public attention in 1914–15 by opposing openly the enlistment of Irishmen in the British army even though the Irish Nationalist party was pledged to support British arms. Britain had other reasons to be suspicious of Sinn Fein. Intelligence was certain that the party's leadership had been infiltrated by the secret revolutionary organization, the Irish Republican Brotherhood (IRB), which was itself the descendant of the similar nineteenth-century terrorist society, the Fenian Brotherhood.

This mistrust was well founded. On Monday of Easter Week, April 24, 1916, the IRB, leading a small force of badly armed men, not more than 1,500 in all, had attempted to overturn the British administration in Dublin. They failed utterly. Unable to capture the seat of government, Dublin Castle, they took only the Post Office in Sackville (now O'Connell) Street, a Poor House, a flour mill, and a few other buildings. By Saturday, April 29, the Easter Rising was all over. What had been planned as a national rising was confined in fact to the center of the capital. The bulk of Dublin, with a civilian population more prosperous during the war than within living memory, seemed to be unmoved. Columns of prisoners herded through the streets were jeered. It was not a revolution, nor even a revolt, wrote the Secretary of State for Ireland, Augustine Birrell, to the Prime Minister immediately after the event, and it would be a pity if it became one.

The Easter Rising came to be, nonetheless, the natal event of the Irish Republic, made so by British cruelty and stupidity in the months that followed. The Cabinet declared martial law, appointed as Commander-in-Chief a hard-bitten, much decorated, Scottish battlefield soldier, General Sir John Maxwell, and failed, in the midst of a European war, to supervise him. Maxwell behaved in Ireland exactly as if he were putting down a riot in a slum quarter of Cairo, a task with which he was long familiar. He took hostages, held hundreds of suspects, and shot, with the approval of the Cabinet, fifteen leaders of the uprising. He permitted, or failed to prevent, a small number of random executions by soldiers. Within two months, by the middle of June 1916, he had made a constitutional settlement in Ireland impossible, the countryside was in arms, and the old Irish Nationalist parliamentary party was all but dead.

In this context Sinn Fein won after all. The new public consensus was apparent in Irish by-elections. In the fifteen months between February 1917, when Lloyd George lifted martial law, and June 1918, the Sinn Fein political party overturned the entrenched Irish Nationalist party six times. Finally, in the general election on December 14, 1918, the revolutionaries won seventy-three of the 103 Irish seats, leaving the Nationalists with only seven. Significantly, the Nationalists were unable even to find candidates for twenty-five of their usual seats. Immediately after the returns were announced, on January 7, 1919, twenty-six of the Sinn Fein MPs, generally being those not in jail, met in Dublin, proclaimed themselves the Parliament of the Republic of Ireland (the *Dáil Eireann*), and formed a government, electing Eamon de Valera, who was himself in jail, as President.

Nonetheless, at the beginning of 1919, Ireland was independent only within its own perception of history. British strength in the island was substantial. There were the national police (the

Royal Irish Constabulary), nominally 10,000 men, although at that time the force was far below establishment. Also present were several divisions of British troops who could be rapidly reinforced. But, on the other hand, with world attention focused on the peace conference about to meet in Paris and on the political convulsions in Central Europe, British policy simply denied the existence of an emergency of any kind. An Irish delegation was declined recognition or seating in Paris and Lloyd George refused to declare martial law. Thus violence was not only likely, but for Sinn Fein necessary. It began in September 1919 with the sack of a village by British soldiers after a local coroner's jury refused to bring any charge against a man accused of murdering a soldier returning from church.

For the next twenty months, Ireland suffered repeated violence, reprisal, and counterviolence of a sort almost unknown in the western world since the Middle Ages. Like the Easter Rising, the events of this time, the "Troubles," are celebrated in Ireland in song and story, and are part of its folk tradition. The reports of British violence against Ireland determined public opinion in Great Britain and in the United States. By the summer of 1920, when the British government had embarked upon what was clearly a program of counterterrorism in Ireland, newspapers in the United States, not to mention American politicians, as well as Liberal newspapers in Britain, were universally condemning army and police behavior. The Royal Irish Constabulary, usually referred to as the "Black and Tans," were invariably named as villains. Technically, the Black and Tans were only the new English recruits hurriedly taken into the much depleted, and hitherto exclusively Irish, ranks of the Royal Irish Constabulary in 1919. Because there were not enough RIC uniforms immediately available, the new men, all former soldiers, temporarily wore army khaki and the forest-green, almost black, RIC billed caps. They were compared derisively to a well-known pack of Kerry foxhounds, the Black and Tans, and have been styled thus ever since. Worse, the RIC had been accused of crimes that were in fact committed by an entirely separate group, the Royal Irish Constabulary Auxiliary (R.I.C.A.). This force, not larger than 1,500, was recruited from former army officers and paid, it was said, the unbelievable wage of one pound per day. They were not part of the old and honorable Royal Irish Constabulary establishment, but were in effect mercenaries, independent contractors, hired guns. Although they wore army uniforms and Glengarry caps and were under army discipline, the R.I.C.A. has been frequently referred to as the "Black and Tans" or simply the "Tans," which is a mistake. After the Irish settlement and with the rise of tension between Jews and Arabs many R.I.C.A. members appear to have gone to Palestine as police for the British mandate government.

During the war, in 1916 immediately after the Easter Rising, again in 1917, and finally again in the late spring of 1918 as a part of the need to extend military conscription to Ireland, the Cabinet had attempted to find some formula for giving a measure of Home Rule to Ireland that all Irish would accept. Each time they reached the same impasse: neither the North nor the South were interested. The Unionists, in Ulster, wanted no devolution of power of any kind; the South, with Sinn Fein now dominating the twenty-six Catholic counties, cared only for complete independence. This intractable balance was seriously disturbed, however, by the Anglo-Irish landowners of the south, the Protestant Ascendancy, usually termed simply the "Ascendancy." This Irish landowning class was neither as numerous nor as wealthy as their counterparts in England, but they were well-represented within Conservative party leadership and in the House of Lords. The Protestant Ascendancy had effortlessly destroyed a delicate compromise proposal negotiated by Lloyd George after the Easter Rising. The difference between the Ascendancy of the South and bitter Protestant Unionists of the North lay in the fact that the Northerners cared little about what happened in the South so long as Ulster was not disturbed. But the Ascendancy could maintain the English connection only with Northern help.

Prime Minister Lloyd George clearly understood this weakness in the Irish anti-Home Rule position and was prepared to exploit it. Late in 1919, the British government announced the Fourth Home Rule Bill, which reproduced by and large the terms of the third bill of 1912—reduced representation at Westminster and a separate parliament and cabinet with jurisdiction over all domestic affairs but religion—except that in place of a single government in Dublin there now would be two, one in Dublin and a second in Belfast.

The Belfast government would have jurisdiction over six of the nine counties of Ulster containing not quite one-and-a-half million people of whom about two-thirds were Protestant. The three western counties of historic Ulster, in which Protestants were a minority, were to be subject to the Dublin government as would the 300,000 or so Protestants in the South.

This was an awkward compromise, which gave neither the largely Protestant North nor the Catholic South what it wanted. It left nearly a half million Catholics in the North and a slightly smaller number of Protestants in the South within the control of governments they detested, a recipe for instability. Yet it accomplished something without which no Irish settlement would have been possible: it destroyed Sinn Fein's basic contention that it, and it alone, represented the will of the Irish people. An elected government in Belfast, however unfairly chosen, could claim for itself the same rights that Sinn Fein had won in the South in the election of 1918.

So it proved. By the beginning of 1921 the repeated cycles of murder, destruction, and reprisal had worn out the Irish Republican Army (IRA), the Lord Mayor of Cork to the world's horror had allowed himself to starve to death in prison, and except among the most uncompromising Unionists, any British sentiment for a policy of suppression had died. After extended negotiations, during which a Northern Ireland Parliament was elected, a military truce was signed in Dublin on July 8, 1921. There followed five months of talks between the British government and representatives of the Dublin provisional government, at first with President De Valera and later with Michael Collins and Arthur Griffith, the founder of Sinn Fein. The difficult story of the negotiation that followed need not be recounted, but in view of the subsequent turbulent history of Northern Ireland a few observations on that province's foundation are in order.

Prime Minister Lloyd George took the trouble for once to address himself completely to Irish affairs, which, he had complained frequently, he had always found time-consuming, squalid, and hateful. He was convinced that despite the separation decreed by the Fourth Home Rule Act, the future of the province of Ulster lay eventually within a united Ireland. Economic considerations alone, he thought, would bring the two sections together. Hence the 1920 act provided for a council to be made up of Members of each Parliament for management of all-island affairs and which could be empowered also to deal with any other matters delegated by either Parliament. But Lloyd George came to realize during the negotiations with Collins and Griffith that Sinn Fein cared for nothing but the union of the thirty-two counties. A twenty-six county government would never be the nation. A settlement without the North would be unstable.

To Lloyd George all of this meant that if a lasting Irish peace were to be achieved, the initiative for union with the South would have to come from Belfast. Constitutionally, Northern Ireland's position was unassailable and British public opinion would never sanction coercion of Ulster. But he could help to begin the process for union. At the beginning of November 1921, Lloyd George suggested privately that the Northern Irish Parliament consider transferring the legislative subordination it owed to London under the Fourth Home Rule Act to the southern government that would emerge from the Treaty negotiations. The connection between Northern Ireland and Great Britain, he pointed out, would remain because Ireland would continue to be in the Empire. (The December 1921 Treaty specified that Southern Ireland would have the same status within the Empire as Canada, in effect a Dominion.) Irish domestic authority would not diminish. The North would simply have Home Rule from Dublin instead of from London. As the greatest inducement, he observed, Northern Ireland's taxes surely would be much lower than if it were attached to Great Britain. The complete proposal, transmitted to the new Prime Minster of Northern Ireland, Sir James Craig, in a letter on November 10, 1921, was supposed to be secret, but it soon became known and evoked fury among senior Unionists. In the territorial settlement Lloyd George had abandoned hundreds of thousands of loyal Protestants to the Catholic South. Now he was trying to bribe the northern province itself to surrender to a union under the southern government. (Although Lloyd George alone was blamed, he had discussed his proposal to Craig with two of the most intransigent members of his circle, Lord Birkenhead and Winston Churchill, both of whom approved.)

As it fell, Griffith and Collins acquiesced. In the early morning hours of December 6, 1921, with expressed misgiving, they accepted the offer of dominion status for twenty-six counties of the south and a divided Ireland. Ireland remained within the Empire, gave up Ulster, and suffered yet another year of civil war, this time from a Sinn Fein rebellion. (Documents released from the Public Record Office only in 1993 show that had the Treaty negotiation failed the British government intended to proclaim martial law at once, use the army to crush Irish resistance, and begin massive internments. The Royal Navy, for example, planned to hold 2,500 men at Scapa Flow.)

But in his negotiations Lloyd George gave up more than is generally realized. The abortive proposal of November 10, with the much more widely known and better understood desertion of the Southern Protestants, must be counted as the major factor in unravelling the tattered fabric of Lloyd George's coalition with the Conservatives. Within months backbench conspiracies against him were widespread even while he retained the loyalty of the Conservative leaders in the Cabinet. Finally, after ten months of unsuccessful foreign policy experiments culminating in a failed British attempt to support Greece's claims in Turkey, which nearly took Britain into war with the Turkish revolutionary government, the Conservative rank and file had had enough. On the morning of October 19, 1922, they declared their independence of the Lloyd George coalition and damned the consequences.

5 / THE BALDWIN ERA

STANLEY BALDWIN,
PRIME MINISTER AND CONSERVATIVE

Between October of 1922 and October of 1931, the British government, in response to the mood of the nation, sought a formula to ensure political stability and settled government. The slogan used by the Conservatives in the general election of November 15, 1922, following Lloyd George's resignation, was "tranquility," which presumably meant political peace and an end to experiment, excitement, and new departures. The Conservative slogan encapsulated the public's nostalgia, their longing for the calm and sunlit afternoons on the croquet lawn and the tea dances in palm courts associated in the public imagination with the Edwardian period.

Over all of this presided the amiable person of Stanley Baldwin, who in 1937 became Earl Baldwin of Bewdley, and whose presence dominated British politics through the central period of this study. He had become Prime Minister on May 22, 1923, when Andrew Bonar Law, afflicted with throat cancer, resigned after just seven months in office. Baldwin, Bonar Law's Chancellor of the Exchequer but an almost unknown figure, was named Prime Minister to the surprise of the political world.

Baldwin is always described as enigmatic, which is quite true. He has no satisfactory biography and, overshadowed by Lloyd George on one side and Neville Chamberlain and Winston Churchill on the other, he is a somewhat misty figure to all but specialists. Even in his time he was a mystery to colleagues. His decisions were private, intuitive, and usually unexplained. He was reluctant, in truth, to make decisions. He was particularly unwilling to resolve disputes among members of his Cabinet, telling them always to find a solution together, the signature of a weak leader. While genial and slow to take offense, he was indolent, although recognized as an assiduous attender of the

House of Commons, in contrast to Lloyd George. He was rather despised by some of the most talented men within his Cabinet of whom the strongest and most important were his immediate successors, Neville Chamberlain and Winston Churchill.

Yet, historically, Stanley Baldwin remains the central figure of the interwar period. During the fourteen years between 1923 and 1937 he was in power, either officially as Prime Minister or effectively as leader of the majority Conservatives in the Commons, for all but three. When he retired in May 1937 after seeing King George VI through the coronation, he was wildly popular. If he had not gained the respect of his colleagues, he clearly embodied the mood of the British people. He was comfortable and reassuring. His pipe, his old-fashioned clothes, his mellow voice (excellent on the new medium for politicians, the radio), his well-upholstered wife, all seemed to represent Englishness and security in an uncertain age.

However behind the public image of everyone's favorite uncle there lurked an acute and crafty political mind with a well-trained sense of danger and an instinct for survival. During his years as Conservative leader Baldwin faced three major political crises—the General Strike of 1926, the banking panic of 1931, and the abdication of 1936. He managed each in the same way: he did nothing and allowed the problem to develop. He was far less concerned with resolving the problem than in ensuring that advantage would accrue to his party and to himself when the calamity occurred. Hence he allowed British coal miners to strike in 1926, at great cost to their union and to the British coal industry, but he turned public opinion against organized labor. In the 1931 financial panic, with a Labour government in power, he declined to allow his party to take part in a national coalition, the price demanded by American banks for the loans necessary to protect the value of British currency. With, one suspects, much help from Neville Chamberlain, he forced the Labour party to split, the government to resign, and Labour to consign itself to a decade of impotent opposition. Finally in 1936, faced with a King who wished to marry a woman who, he was sure, would be an unpopular and unsuitable Queen, he refused either to compromise or to allow Edward VIII to make his case publicly. Edward had no alternative to abdication. The King disappeared as if by magic to be succeeded by his happily married brother. Baldwin had won again.

Baldwin may be generally responsible for finding and carving out the place that the Conservative party has held for the remainder of this century, the normal party of government. At the end of the nineteenth century it had been the party of the Crown and Empire, the land and the Church of England. As World War I approached, with the growth of the demand among many Tories for an end to free trade, the party had acquired a strong element of commerce and industry which traditionally had been Liberal, but it remained also the party of money and prescriptive privilege.

The Conservatives admitted no class bias, but in the years before 1914 they were becoming visibly a party of plutocracy, of business and capitalism. Baldwin understood intuitively that the chaos of war had broken many barriers in British society. The electorate had tripled in 1918. Millions of women and also millions of young soldiers voted for the first time. Party loyalties were loosened or dissolved. Meanwhile Labour had declared itself a party of workers and socialists. The proper Conservative response, he was sure, was to declare in every possible way that the Conservative party, in contrast, was classless and open, and that it welcomed everyone. After becoming party leader in the spring of 1923, he supported steps already taken to enlarge and democratize party organization. Perhaps more important, he repeatedly warned other party leaders—Winston Churchill, who had rejoined the party in 1924 as Chancellor of the Exchequer, and Neville Chamberlain, the coming man—to suppress their antitrade union rhetoric. He stifled, not by opposition but by benign neglect, a well-organized movement among a number of older party grandees to give back power to a reconstructed House of Lords. He strongly supported the establishment of constituency labor organizations. Most of all, in his own speeches, he reminded Britons by allusion and illustration that they were one people, that class antagonism was foreign and detestable, and that England should be merry and compassionate, not a barracks commanded by dreary socialist doctrinaires.

Indeed friendly compassion in place of class warfare provided the continuing theme of Baldwin's attack upon Labour. Whether he truly believed his own rhetoric cannot be known. Certainly his stories of old mill hands drawing wages at his father's Baldwin Iron Works long after their usefulness had disappeared were true. But it is equally clear that he had no compunction about using his very considerable negotiating skills to thwart and embarrass organized labor in 1926, while in 1931 he nearly destroyed the Labour party in the House of Commons.

Those who remember Baldwin think of him as a peacemaker. Without his meliorative presence Britain could have seen the revolution in the late twenties or early thirties that occurred in so many other countries in Europe. It is also true that in the years between 1931 and 1933 when the Great Depression swept over the world and most industrial nations turned to radical idealogues of the left or right, Britain clung firmly to the reassuring and distinctly unradical figure of Stanley Baldwin.

BALDWIN AND LABOUR, CHAMBERLAIN AND SOCIAL REFORM

Baldwin's accession to the Prime Ministership in May 1923 coincided almost exactly with the occupation by the French army, with some Belgian contingents, of the valley of the Ruhr River between Essen and Dortmund in Germany. This area was the heart of German steel making and coal mining. The French announced they would extract the Ruhr's wealth for the payment of reparations upon which Germany had defaulted. The German government responded by calling upon all workers in the Ruhr valley to strike. All of this caused disastrous inflation in Germany, destroying all savings and also wiping out the German government's mammoth domestic war debt, but it ended for a year German coal exports. World coal prices leaped up by 20 percent and British coal production increased accordingly.

The effect of this increase in production was to reverse the decline in the British coal industry that had begun with the price collapse in 1920 and had culminated in the bitter and unsuccessful strike of 1921. The miners again became militant. In 1924, as Baldwin returned to power after the first, impotent and short, Labour administration, the Miners' Federation again threatened industrial action. Ominously the miners were supported in their demands by the other two members of the so-called Triple Alliance, the railway union and the General Workers' Union, which were, with the miners, the largest labor organizations in the nation. A strike by the Triple Alliance would paralyze the country.

However, by the time Baldwin assumed office a second time, in November 1924, the Ruhr occupation had ended, German miners were back at work, and world coal prices had collapsed a second time. After complicated negotiations, the British government agreed in July 1925 to subsidize the coal industry for nine months, until April 30, 1926, and to appoint a second Royal Commission to examine the condition of the coal industry and the possibilities for its nationalization.

The key to the understanding of all conversations between the government and the coal unions, by no means unknown to economic historians, but insufficiently emphasized, turns on the fact that the miners' union after the war was determined to force government ownership of the coal industry. The Miners' Federation was as aware as anyone that coal use was declining and that the industry would never be profitable again overall. An individual mine, a new one with a broad and tall coal face, could perhaps make money. But energy production, particularly for shipping, had turned to oil. The demand for Welsh bunker coal for ships would never recover. Private owners would not invest for the replacement of out-of-date machinery in a dying industry. The only solution was public ownership.

The underlying motive for the miners' intransigence lay then in their determination to force nationalization. Toward this end, the mines' continued unprofitability was a weapon; the owners would be happy to accept the guaranteed income from government bonds in place of highly uncertain coal profits. To the miners, coal was a livelihood. To the owners, it was a sick investment, although they did not say so. The government could save both. Mines were needed to provide jobs, not coal. Hence the miners refused even to discuss either reductions in wage rates or increases in hours worked. "Not a penny off the pay, not a minute on the day," served as the slogan.

The result was a complete impasse in negotiation. The Royal Commission reported at the beginning of March 1926 and pointedly did not recommend nationalization. Its report sold nearly 100,000 copies, which may be a measure of the gravity with which the British public regarded the approaching general strike. On April 30 the government subsidy expired and the next morning lockout notices appeared at the pit heads. The miners' strike began. The serious question now was what the other unions would do.

Viewed in perspective it is reasonably clear that Baldwin did nothing to prevent a general strike. He was sure a political strike—one not for economic advantage but for a political goal, nationalization—would anger not only the British middle class but many workers as well. Accordingly, he did not even try to dissuade the trade union leaders from supporting the miners. On Sunday evening, May 2, he simply retired from negotiations and went to bed. At midnight the next day most work in Britain stopped.

The General Strike lasted only nine days and in the literal sense was not general. Only about three quarters of the 4,000,000 members of the Trades Union Congress were called out. Factories closed, but for the ordinary citizen the most visible effect was the cessation of newspapers, of all public transport, and of food distribution. The latter services were partly restored by the substitution of volunteers and by the use of the army to bring in food. Indeed it is the efficient preparation of an emergency volunteer organization for policing and for transportation that provides the best evidence that Baldwin expected and accepted— welcomed might be too strong a word—a national strike. When asked later why he had given the special wage subsidy announced in the summer of 1925, he replied simply: "We were not ready." In the spring of 1926, he was prepared.

Although the nine-day General Strike was unimportant as an economic event, the coal strike that had caused it dragged on for six months. When, as in the 1921 coal strike, the miners were starved into submission and agreed to return at reduced wages, nearly 200,000 had no jobs to which to go. (Coal employment was 1,115,000 in March 1926 before the strike and 943,000 in December 1926 after it. While there was some revival in 1927, which was the most prosperous year between 1920 and 1939, in 1928 coal employment was down to 939,000. Put another way, unemployment in the mining industry went from 9.5 percent in 1926 to 23.6 percent by 1928.) The General Strike is therefore a critical episode in the long and sad decline of the once proud British coal industry.

On the other hand the collapse of the General Strike, amounting essentially to the abandonment of the miners by the rest of the labor movement, demonstrates the essential conservatism, the British orderliness, of the working class. Baldwin, on May 3, had called the strike unconstitutional and within the terms of the undiluted conventionality of his mind, so it was. Since 1918, all British workers, like everyone else, had been represented in the House of Commons. There was no rule in the land above the enactments of a lawful Parliament. No one could appeal from it. Yet this was the intent of the strikers. Over the head of Parliament they were trying to coerce the nation into political action, into nationalization.

These ideas, when enunciated in the House of Commons in simple, homely language by Baldwin and in precise legal language by Sir John Simon of the Liberals, made an impression, not least upon the leaders of the other two unions of the Triple Alliance, J. H. Thomas and Ernest Bevin. Without their two huge organizations, the railwaymen and the General Workers' Union, a General Strike could not continue.

Everyone knew that moderate trade union leaders had been desperate to end the strike from the moment it began. In nine days, on May 12, with very little negotiation and nothing on paper except a highly unspecific agreement to do something for the coal miners, who felt themselves betrayed, the General Strike ended. Baldwin himself had not taken part. He had asked the nation over the BBC (British Broadcasting Corporation) simply to trust him.

The settlement made Baldwin a hero. As he would do just ten years later in the affair of Edward VIII's abdication, he had forced a settlement by his own inertia. He had convinced his opponents not only that his, Baldwin's, point of view represented the will of the nation but that it was morally right. Having done that he let events take their course.

Although it was not then apparent, Baldwin had also solidified his premiership, having succeeded Bonar Law as an unknown. Baldwin's short first administration from May 1923 to January 1924 was undistinguished and dominated by his controversial proposal to reintroduce tariffs as a way to combat unemployment. His first Cabinet contained little talent and much inexperience. It was a second-class team. His next ministry, on the other hand, contained one past and two future Prime Ministers as well as other men of talent, some with many more years Cabinet service than Baldwin had. A number of the most brilliant of these men, Winston Churchill, F. E. Smith, Earl of Birkenhead, and Neville Chamberlain, had urged war on labor. Baldwin had desisted, allowing labor to destroy itself. His method had been proven right, and theirs wrong.

Finally, the easy defeat of the General Strike ended for a decade organized labor's dominion over British economic life, which it had gained during the war. People were no longer afraid of labor power. Labor's terrifying boasts about its ability to bring commerce and industry to a stop did not mean so much. After the strike, membership in the Trades Union Congress dropped by about three hundred thousand in 1927 and by the same amount again in 1928 and would not reach four million again until 1937.

All of this is not to say that the Labour party as a political force was seriously weakened. It is possible to argue that as union militancy was contained, the fear of Labour irresponsibility in office, which had been genuine and widespread before 1924, evaporated for all but partisan purposes. So Labour became more electable, while the Conservatives were not invulnerable. Baldwin's popularity was his own, turning upon his real friendliness and his old-fashioned way of saying nothing sonorously. He attracted loyalty from voters who felt they knew him intimately, but this regard was for him alone and was not transferable to the government or the Conservative party as a whole.

Nonetheless, as it approached the end of its statutory five-year parliamentary term, Baldwin's government could regard the coming election of 1929 with some confidence. In their favor, there was of course the personal popularity of Prime Minister Baldwin, the peacemaker and healer, but beyond this there was a solid record of Conservative achievement. The Treasury had restored the pound's convertibility to gold at the prewar rate of one pound to $4.86, a move warmly applauded in the banking community and one that seemed to the rest of the population, so far as they understood it, to signify the restoration of the City of London as the financial capital of the world. What lay unremarked upon by the general public was that gold convertibility at the old rate made British products at least 10 percent more expensive in world markets than they should have been. It also made the country's huge war debt harder to manage and ran contrary to the general trend among most of Britain's competitors of paying off war costs and modernizing industry by inflation. Britain managed a feeble prosperity between 1925 and 1929 because the rest of the world was wildly prosperous and hungry for its goods. The disastrous consequence of the revival of the gold standard would become clear only after the world depression began in the 1930s. But in the complaisant days of the late twenties the "return to gold," except for the carping of a few college professors, seemed to be a triumph and a readjustment of the last dislocation of the war.

Baldwin's government had accomplished more. Its most successful member, clearly the coming man, was Arthur Neville Chamberlain, the Minister of Health. He was the son of the mighty Joseph Chamberlain who had begun the reformation of the Conservative party that Baldwin completed. Neville Chamberlain was Baldwin's opposite in mind and in work habits, in public behavior, and indeed in appearance. He was businesslike and practical in his work, terse in conversation, short-tempered, selfconfident, and utterly contemptuous of the Labour party. He was tall, thin, and impatient of contradiction, maintaining a sour face even when he tried to smile. He looked, observed Winston Churchill, as if he had been weaned on a pickle. Not surprisingly, in the Conservative-dominated administration that would take office later, in 1931, he became a Chancellor of the Exchequer of almost legendary efficiency, the best Chancellor, it was said, since Gladstone.

Chamberlain was easily the most accomplished legislative craftsman of Baldwin's second cabinet. In 1925 he put into the statute book a huge and complicated contributory pension act, something that his father and Lloyd George each had tried and failed to do before the war. In 1929 he completely overhauled both the Poor Law and local government's system of taxation and grants-in-aid. That Chamberlain, stiff, unsympathetic, the ideal Permanent Secretary who became the Mandarin Prime Minister, should be the most energetic and successful social reformer of the interwar period says much about the concerns of the ordinary British voter and still more about the leadership of the Labour party. Between his two accomplishments in 1925 and 1929, Chamberlain put into place a mass of boring and complex, but useful, reform in the administration of health insurance, Poor Law, and local government activity, both increasing efficiency and saving money. For him good government was nothing more than good administration. The structure of the modern British welfare state owes as much to the remedial work of the unpleasant Minister of Health of the 1920s as to the imaginative first architect of national insurance, David Lloyd George.

The Conservatives approached the 1929 election with a good deal of equanimity. Chamberlain's work had been necessary and farreaching. It should have been popular, but of course, it was not. Nor did the Conservatives receive any due credit for extending the vote in 1928 to all women between twenty-one and thirty-one. The party's only drawing card was Stanley Baldwin himself. He became the feature of the Conservative campaign. The Prime Minister's picture and the not particularly daring slogans "Trust Baldwin" and "Safety First" constituted the Conservative platform for the polling that finally was set for May 30, 1929.

By contrast, Labour offered a platform that would become its staple from the 1920s on: higher, but unspecific, taxes upon the rich, higher welfare benefits, more public housing, and nationalization of "basic" industry. Paradoxically, its unadventurous administration in 1924 had given it some respectability as a possible alternative government. Beyond a small but useful reform of Lloyd George's public housing program, putting local authorities permanently into the business of providing working class living accommodations, and its tentative approaches to the Soviet Union which resulted in the government's dismissal, Labour's first nine months under Ramsay MacDonald had accomplished nothing. Under no circumstances could a party that had done so little be considered revolutionary.

For the Liberal party, the 1929 election was critical; it would be victory or farewell. In 1926, partly as a result of differences with Lloyd George over the General Strike, Herbert Asquith had retired as leader, to die two years later. For the first time in a decade the party had a single chief, although to say that it was united, as Clement Attlee wickedly put it, would mean only that its members were at one in the mistrust of their leader. Still, if they were to regain their place as the accepted opposition to the Conservatives, a potential governing party, the Liberals had to do well on May 30, 1929. Although somehow they failed to understand it, their enemy was not the comfortable person of Stanley Baldwin, but Labour.

The Liberals seemed determined to seek their own extinction and to promote the Labour party. While most Liberal voters in the absence of a candidate of their own would support a Conservative, the party leadership maintained the fiction that Labour was an ally and Conservatism the enemy. Repeatedly in the coming years hopeless Liberal candidates intervened in narrowly held Conservative seats to draw off their party's Conservative supporters so to throw the seat to Labour.

In 1929, the Liberals produced for the last time in their history a full slate of candidates who were supported by plenty of money. Moreover, the party had in hand a well-thought-out series of plans for treating Britain's multiple economic problems including, for example, an analysis of the coal industry, produced in 1924, that virtually predicted the general strike of 1926.

It was all to no avail. On May 30, despite the massive effort and a decent response from the electorate which gave them 5,000,000 votes as opposed to 8,000,000 for the other two parties, the Liberals seated only fifty-nine Members of Parliament. Labour won twenty-eight more seats than the Conservatives even though Baldwin's party collected nearly 300,000 more votes than Labour and a higher percentage of votes per candidate. While the Liberals held the balance of power in the new Parliament, the day of the ancient Liberal party as a front-bench, independent, political force was over, and the Labour party leader, Ramsay McDonald, was to form a second Cabinet.

THE ECONOMIC BLIZZARD, THE CRISIS OF 1931

At the end of his first administration, Baldwin, after being defeated in the middle of November 1923, had waited upon the assembly of Parliament in January 1924 before resigning on a motion of no confidence. In 1929 he resigned immediately, and on June 5, James Ramsay MacDonald took office again as Prime Minister.

No man could have been more unlucky, even one who had risen from the abject poverty of a fatherless childhood in Lossiemouth, Scotland, to the place of the King's First Minister. MacDonald was a selftaught intellectual with some of the arrogant defensiveness of personality that often accompanies that extraction. Neither a university radical nor trade union functionary, he had entered trade union politics at its beginning in 1900 as secretary of the Labour Representation Committee. He became Chairman of the Labour party in 1911, but resigned after the war broke out. After serving some time in jail for opposing conscription during the war, he became again leader of the Parliamentary Labour party in 1922.

Three months after the new government took office the American stock market, having enjoyed an uninterrupted rise for nearly a year and a half, began to falter. Then in the last week of October 1929, in a series of sickening plunges starting on October 23, the Wall Street stock market fell apart. By the middle of November the Dow industrial average was exactly one-half the figure of early September. At its nadir on July 8, 1932, the thirty Dow industrials stood at fifty-eight.

The great stock market crash was a result of the preceding decade of American prosperity and industrial expansion, in which Britain had not participated. For Britain the immediate effect of the Wall Street collapse was the disappearance of new American deposits in the British banking system and the beginning of an almost frantic repatriation to the United States of loans and portfolio investments already made. Funds that had been flowing into the City (the London financial district) for years now began to flow out in an ever-growing torrent. In London the effect was a violent contraction in the availability of credit, making difficult the continuation of loans to European banks, where the City's international banking community had done much of its business since 1924. The loss of credit from the United States left Britain vulnerable, particularly to any problems in the German banking community.

The second blow to the British economy from the United States arrived nine months after the stock market crash with President Herbert Hoover's signing of the Hawley-Smoot tariff bill raising the average *ad valorem* rate on dutiable imports into the United States to 53.2 percent and causing a virtual prohibition on the import of many commodities.

Hawley-Smoot was a singular catastrophe for Britain because since the war America had become again the largest foreign consumer of British exports, although ironically Britain imported about three times as much from the United States as it exported to it. In 1928 Britain sold £69,000,000 worth of goods, exports and reexports, to the United States. In 1932 the figure was £21,000,000. The Hawley-Smoot tariff served efficiently to export the American depression to the United Kingdom.

London's financial problems demonstrated the fragility of Britain's credit position and the futility of the return to gold in 1925 as if nothing had changed since 1914. British banking was now having to operate with borrowed funds, mostly American. The City's own liquidity had been dissipated during the war in the purchase of American munitions. Britain was now at the mercy of its own debtors. By 1930, exports to the United States were 42 percent less than 1928. By 1932 they would fall by as much again.

Hence the MacDonald administration, before it had been in office a year, was faced by a domestic economic calamity brought on by world conditions over which it had absolutely no control. In Britain the rule of thumb always had been that two out of every five workers were employed by consumers abroad. Trade began to falter in the winter of 1929–30 and by March 1930 unemployment had grown by 400,000, i.e. 30 percent, over the previous March to 1,600,000. It could be noted that this was before the Hawley-Smoot tariff was enacted in June. By the end of 1930, 2,600,000, well over 20 percent of all insured workers, were without jobs.

Unemployment brought the second stage of the crisis. Out-of-work benefits, seventeen shillings per week, were technically paid from an unemployment insurance fund supported by contributions from those at work. The ratio between contributions and benefits assumed an average of 6 percent unemployment. However in times of exceptional unemployment when the fund was depleted, the administrators were entitled to borrow from the Treasury. So the cost of support for the one-fifth of the British workforce without jobs fell ultimately upon the budget. By the beginning of 1931 the Treasury was advancing the unemployment fund £1,000,000 per week and was raiding the City banking system and money market to finance a growing budget deficit.

Admittedly these sums were not large in terms of customary City business. But banking is built upon confidence in a stable economic environment and upon an accepted political system. Indeed, it depends upon the good faith of the bank's customer, a fact not always understood by the customer. Without good faith, fiduciary investments, that is deposits and credit, do not work. MacDonald's government of 1929–31 had the confidence neither of its own party in the House of Commons, which found it insufficiently radical, nor of the rest of Britain's, and the world's, business communities which doubted both Labour's financial dexterity and its prudence.

The looming crisis finally exploded on May 11, 1931, when the Rothschild bank in Vienna, the *Kredit Anstalt*, suspended gold payments. Ironically this action was the result, not of economic conditions, but of the defalcation of some of the officers. But the result was the same. The Austrian government shut all banks and forbade the export of specie. Because Vienna served as the money center for much of south Germany the effect of the Austrian moratorium was simply to transfer the banking emergency to Germany. With their liquidity frozen German banks now began to close and on July 15, 1931, in order to protect its own system, the German government prohibited the export of gold or currency.

For Britain then the critical date was July 15. The classical banking stratagem of beggar-your-creditor now brought the German crisis to the City whose largest creditor was the United States to which speculators were already frantically withdrawing gold across the Atlantic. Britain's exposure in Germany and Austria amounted to £90,000,000. On July 15 the price of British sterling in New York fell like a stone. In the last weeks of July the flow out of London became a torrent. On July 28 the Bank of England borrowed £50,000,000 in the Paris and New York money markets and on August 6 the Bank reported that in the last four weeks alone it had lost £60,000,000 in gold trying to protect the British banking system.

In the first three weeks of August 1931 then, the international payment difficulties, which so far had been entirely an economic problem confined to banks, became a political problem. The budget emergency brought on by ever-mounting unemployment and the banking-currency crisis joined together to cause a towering political crisis that would destroy the Labour government, while coming close to ruining the Labour party. In the process, the Conservatives returned to control the House of Commons, a dominion they would retain for the next fourteen years.

The facts of the situation were simple enough. First, the deficit for the current fiscal year, four months old in July, would be, without economies, £170,000,000. The greatest drain on the Treasury, according to the Chancellor of the Exchequer, Philip Snowden, was the cost of unemployment benefits, £143,000,000. Second, by mid-August the proceeds of the first loan of £50,000,000 were already gone. It was clear a new larger loan was necessary although this time it would have to be on the credit of the British government. The sums were too large for interbank transfers. Third, after enquiring at the Federal Reserve Bank of New York on August 13, the MacDonald Cabinet was told that while a loan of, say, £100,000,000 could certainly be raised in New York such accommodation would not be forthcoming until there was a substantial program of economy "receiving the full approval of parliament." In communications during the next few days it became clear that this stipulation did not mean a mere trimming of the edges of the budget, nor would New York be satisfied by a pious declaration from party leaders about the joys of money-saving. What the New York banks really wanted was a coalition government in Britain. But without the cooperation of the Conservatives there would be no coalition government without which there would be no loan. Yet without a loan Britain's international credit would disappear.

On August 19 the Labour Cabinet had met to consider possible cuts in the budget. At this time the division between the rules of fiscal responsibility and the imperatives of social justice became starkly apparent. Although there was some reluctant agreement on certain economies within the civil service, the Cabinet majority could find savings of only £28,500,000 in unemployment insurance and more than half of this would come from an increase in the contribution by those still at work. No one, except presumably MacDonald, Snowden, and J. H. Thomas, was willing to touch the seventeen-shilling unemployment benefit itself. Labour would not sell its soul to rescue the Bank of England. Snowden had announced on August 20 that unemployment insurance alone would probably cost £143,000,000.

When Parliament recessed on August 1 Baldwin had retreated to Aix-les-Bains in France. He came back to London briefly at the height of the bank panic and finding nothing to interest him, returned to France. One may assume he spoke with Neville Chamberlain. Accordingly it was with Chamberlain, who regarded all Labour party members as venal or ignorant or both, that MacDonald and Snowden had to deal.

The MacDonald government was at the mercy of the Conservatives when the two Labour leaders met Chamberlain and Herbert Samuel of the Liberals on August 20. Here, according to the Prime Minister's report to the Cabinet, Chamberlain intimated that £100,000,000 in cuts in unemployment insurance would probably be about the price Labour would have to pay to secure Conservative party political support for a coalition and the foreign loans that would follow. Labour would have not only to sell its ideals but commit immediate suicide as well. (On the same day the General Council of the Trades Union Congress announced unhelpfully that the only cuts in spending it would accept were in the salaries of judges and Cabinet ministers.)

There is no need to follow the agony of the Labour Cabinet and its Prime Minister between August 20 and August 23 when the new government appeared. MacDonald shuttled back and forth between his miserable Labour colleagues and the implacable Neville Chamberlain. The issues were palpable. The American bankers demanded all party support, meaning support from Conservatives. Baldwin, through Chamberlain, demanded a reduction of unemployment insurance. Labour would have to deny its own principles. Chamberlain had foreseen this dilemma in July. He urged his party's leader not to surrender too easily.

The end of Labour's tenure came on Sunday, August 23 when MacDonald reported to the King that there was no chance that the full Cabinet, let alone the Labour party or the Trades Union Congress executive, would accept the cuts in expenditure necessary to purchase the cooperation of the Conservatives. But without these there would be no loans from the United States. He warned that he must resign. Either at MacDonald's suggestion or on his own initiative, the King proposed a consultation of party leaders. Baldwin, unwillingly back from France, and Herbert Samuel of the Liberals each saw the King that day. MacDonald made another attempt to convince the Cabinet that evening of the necessity of unemployment insurance reductions and having failed resigned after midnight. At noon the next day, after another all-party conference a new, "National," government was announced. MacDonald as Prime Minister and three other colleagues, supported by fewer than a dozen so-called "National Labour" members of the House of Commons, remained the only Labour members in the Cabinet. Within weeks all had been expelled from the Labour party for betraying Labour principles.

By the end of September, the crisis had ended in a way that tells more about the implacable conventionality of the Treasury and the British banking community than it does about their financial expertise. The new National government immediately reduced the unemployment benefit to fifteen shillings and the American loan for which the Labour government had been sacrificed duly arrived on September 8. But within ten days the new loan's proceeds had vanished into the pockets of speculators. One wonders who would have expected otherwise. A bet against a currency under pressure is virtually risk-free. At 12:01 in the morning of Monday September 21, Britain ended the gold convertibility of the pound (thought essential to Britain's world trade), no doubt forever. Parliament approved the action that afternoon.

With the end of gold convertibility the payment crisis disappeared like magic. The pound-dollar ratio, of course, declined immediately from $4.86 to $3.58 for a pound, but in Britain prices barely moved. Indeed in the next year they declined slightly and between 1932 and 1939 Britain enjoyed its last period of price stability. More important for the government, without the need to attract gold or foreign investment now that the international value of the pound was set only by the law of supply and demand for the currency, there was no need for an artificially high interest rate. Interest rates could find their efficient, or market clearing, level. In effect importers and consumers, rather than banks, would absorb the pressure on the pound. Bank rates promptly sank from 6 percent to $2^1/2$ percent, the latter rate not seen in Britain since 1909. By the next year it was down to 2 percent, unknown in Britain since the nineteenth century. In 1932 the competent Neville Chamberlain, as Chancellor of the Exchequer, refinanced the war debt (in effect exchanging old high-interest, high-yielding bonds for new low-yielding bonds), saving British taxpayers hundreds of millions of pounds over the years. Of more immediate consequence, borrowing of money by the public moved from being expensive to being cheap. Private housebuilding, of which there had been little in the 1920s, doubled in the 1930s even while Chamberlain cut back severely on the construction of public housing. So far as Britain recovered from the depression in the early 1930s, domestic house construction was probably the catalyst. And briefly, until 1933 when the United States ended gold convertibility and devalued its dollar, British prices, in real, unadjusted terms, were lower for Americans than they had been since before the war, causing a modest influx of United States visitors with their children.

To the economic historian, the mystery arises from the question of why the effects of abandoning the gold standard had not been foreseen. On the contrary, during the August crisis the Chancellor of the Exchequer, Philip Snowden, a man with a considerable, and clearly undeserved, reputation as an economist, had lectured the Cabinet repeatedly on the disasters that would accompany the suspension of the gold standard. He claimed that the price of imports and interest rates would soar, the British standard of living would sink by one-third, and so on. No one in the Labour Cabinet knew enough of the workings of international finance to argue.

Baldwin had again maintained his position through inertia. Even after his reluctant return from Aix-les-Bains on Sunday, August 23, he had kept out of sight so that the King's summons to Buckingham Palace took some time to reach him. He declined to take responsibility for the inevitable crash of sterling it was assumed would occur. He had, he insisted, no interest in becoming Prime Minister himself and demanded repeatedly that MacDonald should stay on.

The new National Government composed of National Labour ministers as well as Conservatives, Liberals, and Liberal Nationals (as opposed to 'National Liberals', who were the Lloyd George Liberal supporters in 1918) won an immense majority in a general election on October 27, 1931. Together the coalition captured 554 seats in a House of Commons then of 615. At the dissolution Labour had held 281 seats. After the election it was left with 52. Moreover, except for Arthur Henderson, its most seasoned and talented leaders, MacDonald, Philip Snowden, and J.H. Thomas, had been expelled from the party. The House of Commons does not work well with a feeble and irresponsible opposition, as the next eight years would show.

DRAWING IN THE ECONOMIC HORNS

In the new government, the active sponsor of policies, was neither Baldwin nor MacDonald, but the Chancellor of the Exchequer, Neville Chamberlain. He possessed nothing but contempt for Labour as a party in the House of Commons, but his terse and practical mind, as well as the political philosophy inherited from his father, made it impossible for him to ignore the working class. To him, social reform and sound, economical administration were not only compatible, they were necessary to each other. "High rates and a healthy city" had been Joseph Chamberlain's slogan when Mayor of Birmingham in the mid-1870s. His son, Neville Chamberlain, Mayor of Birmingham himself in 1915–16, meant to apply this excellent formula to the nation at large. In 1934 he restored the unemployment benefit to the seventeen shillings at which it had stood before the crisis of 1931. By that time seventeen shillings was worth even more than in 1931 because retail prices had fallen by 3 percent. Meanwhile he raised the standard rate of income tax to five shillings in the pound (25 percent), a rate higher than Labour had ever dared attempt, and began a complete overhaul of the unemployment insurance program which was finally put into law as the Unemployment Act of 1934.

Probably Chamberlain's largest project was the destruction of the policy of free trade that had governed Britain's commercial relations with the rest of the world since 1846 with the introduction of a general system of protective tariffs on imports with preferences toward the Dominions and Empire. In this initiative he did not, of course, work alone. A large and constantly growing segment of the Conservative party had been demanding a return to protection since Joseph Chamberlain had first proposed it three decades earlier. Moreover Baldwin, as has been described, had raised the issue in 1923, losing the Prime Ministership as a consequence. Finally, the depression had made the world protectionist. Germany, which had caused the 1931 exchange crisis, was in chaos, dumping goods into Britain while buying little. The infamous Hawley-Smoot tariff had nearly eliminated exports to the United States. So far as there had been a concrete issue debated in the election of 1931, aside from the outrage over Ramsay McDonald's treason, it had centered upon trade protection. Still the reintroduction of general tariffs with imperial preferences, even if the program were less perfectly systematic than he would have wished, represented for Chamberlain a triumph not only for himself, but for his family. It was, as he believed, a vindication of his father.

The end of free trade may have seemed only a natural step in political evolution, a belated recognition that Britain was no longer the only workshop of the world, but it marked a significant alteration of the nation's place in the global economy. Combined with the departure from gold convertibility, protection and preference for goods from the Empire together advertised the fact that Britain's worldwide economic dominion no longer existed. In its place there was a restricted trading and currency bloc, still huge to be sure, but made up of nations with which Britain had political connections: either *de jure*, as the dominions and Empire, or *de facto*, as Egypt.

Before the war the western world had possessed in gold a common currency. In practice this meant that any industrial nation's paper money, whether bank notes in the pocket or certificates of credit, could be exchanged for gold which, for technical reasons, did not vary more than 2 percent on either side of the gold value of the nation's standard medium. In normal times (and the word normal must be emphasized) this exchange was seldom required. The pound, the mark, the franc, and the dollar were all literally as good as gold.

This system had made London the huge business and commercial center that it was. A foreign, perhaps a Japanese, importer would routinely maintain a balance at a British bank in British pounds. He would use them, as if they were gold, to pay for goods from, say, the United States. Pounds, dollars, and any other Western currency had a common denominator in gold. For practical purposes they were all the same currency. International trade, even when the traders were not British, was routinely carried on in pounds. There was more. Importers had their creditworthiness "accepted," i.e. certified, in London, payments were settled in London banks, insurance was bought there. These smooth operations, British financial and political leaders had been convinced for well over a century, depended upon the stability and convertibility of the pound sterling. For this reason in 1925, at much cost to British manufacturing, not to mention British workers, the Treasury had restored gold exchange at the old rate. But in 1931 Britain had gone off the gold standard a second time. The value of the pound in terms of dollars had fallen by one-third and its price would in the future be determined not by its value in gold but by the supply of and demand for pounds on the international money markets. And with the gold standard had gone free trade as well. As the pound sterling had been the world's currency, the British Empire had been the world's marketplace. The two together had symbolized, and reciprocally had supported, Britain's economic preeminence. London had been a great warehouse: anything the world produced, whether services or goods, cargo space or racehorse insurance, fine silver flatware or railroad locomotives, could be bought, or sold, in London. But now that was over.

The economic realignment of Britain that occurred in the years between 1931 and 1939 was less a conscious government policy than a piecemeal response to Britain's altered position in the world. What it amounted to was a concentration by Britain on domestic and Imperial markets for trade, coupled with the promotion of the pound as the reserve currency within the Empire and in certain other dependent countries. This latter group, using the pound as a trading currency, was the so-called sterling bloc. Those nations within the bloc were invited to link the value of their currencies to the pound, while Britain would undertake to keep the pound freely convertible. In effect, within the sterling bloc the pound would have the place of gold. At the same time, London hoped to remain the ordinary resort for Imperial needs in banking, insurance, and shipping services. Finally, the bloc would be reinforced by the substantial tariff preferences extended to colonial products entering the British market, above all food, while the colonies would reciprocate with lower duties for British products. The European Union is working toward precisely this system in the 1990s. A preferential tariff community works best with a common currency.

Government's response to Britain's diminished economic position appeared in the more deliberate policy of rebuilding, behind the recently constructed wall of tariffs, its industrial plant, known as "rationalization." This was an obvious reaction to the loss of markets that had occurred in World War I. There existed a clear need for the reduction of capacity, accompanied by the modernization, of the old heavy metal industries, most importantly steel and shipbuilding. Elderly shipyards and steel mills were bought out by funds from a tax on sales of more modern firms and closed. There were workers' protests. The shutting down of Palmer's famous shipyards at Jarrow for example resulted in a book, *The Town They Killed,* and a march of the unemployed to No. 10 Downing Street, the Prime Minister's residence, where Baldwin, characteristically, was unavailable. But the effects of rationalization were important later. The new investment, the modernization of equipment and indeed even the release of redundant labor that took place in the 1930s forced some of Britain's most old-fashioned heavy industries into the twentieth century. Although this was done in the name of international competitiveness, economic historians have questioned whether Britain could have held out in the Second World War had not the improvements been made.

On the other hand, the dislocation caused by restructuring, by the running down of the coal mines and, ironically, by the rise of new light manufacturing and service industries that employed mostly unskilled men and women, all conspired to increase and maintain the high level of unemployment among skilled working men. Unemployment in the 1930s was on the average twice that of the 1920s, a decade that itself was remembered as a period of hard times. The monthly unemployment figures in the thirties hovered around 2,000,000 insured workers registered out of work, close to 20 percent of the workforce, as opposed to 1,000,000 in the earlier decade. Worse, these figures must be considered a minimum. There were hundreds of thousands more, uncounted and uncountable, out of work but unregistered. Having given up the active search for employment they were not included in the registered unemployment figures.

The sufferings of the thirties constitute a fixture of British working class folklore and a determinant of behavior for the next half century. Voters in the general election of 1945 voted against the hardship of the thirties and against Baldwin and Neville Chamberlain who were seen to have presided over these years. Any credit Winston Churchill might have earned for helping to win the war became irrelevant. More than this, however, the thirties made worker security in all its forms the central doctrine of the Labour party. The hysterical public welcome given the Beveridge plan for social insurance in December 1942 illustrates the orientation of the public mind three years before the end of the war. In 1944 the House of Commons agreed, by resolution, that it was the duty of the government to maintain a high and stable level of employment.

But probably most important, the concentration on security of employment made nationalization of industry the central plank of the Labour party platforms. To be sure, government ownership of all major industry—sometimes referred to grandly as "the commanding heights"—had been a staple of socialist doctrine for nearly a century, but after the thirties it became a serious matter. This doctrine should not be confused with "social ownership," or "guild socialism," in effect ownership by the workers themselves, a doctrine which lurked about the intellectual fringes of Labour for years. The Labour party of course had always espoused the slogans of full employment and social security. These were worthy objectives, but they did not translate into a political platform and inconveniently the Conservatives supported the same things. Hence, public ownership of industry (nationalization) emerged as one of the few propositions upon which all schools of party doctrine could agree. It separated Labour from the Conservatives. Unfortunately it also helped to prevent the shrinkage of unprofitable enterprise: coal for example, or railroads, or shipyards, or the docks. The maintenance of employment was more important than profitability. In the half century after the great depression, nationalization almost alone came to mean British socialism.

THE KING'S GREAT CAUSE

In June 1935, under pressure from the Conservative party, particularly from Chamberlain, Stanley Baldwin pushed aside Ramsay Macdonald, who was gradually losing his memory and power of speech, and again assumed the Prime Ministership. He confirmed his leadership in a general election on November 14 in which the Conservatives won 432 seats and MacDonald's National Labour party was nearly destroyed. MacDonald himself was heavily defeated as was his son Malcolm. Labour, still in chaos, revived to 154 MPs.

The last great problem of Baldwin's three administrations erupted little more than two months later when King George V died on January 20, 1936, to be succeeded by his son "David" (his name within the family), the Prince of Wales, who took the title of Edward VIII.

The story of the abdication of King Edward after only 325 days on the throne has been told many times, usually as the drama of Mrs. Simpson—the designing woman, determined to be Queen, who traps a willful, not overly intelligent, forty-year-old bachelor with the selfish, reckless, temperament of a child. That during the past fifteen years Edward had enjoyed great popularity with the British, Canadian, and indeed American, public probably enhanced these troubling aspects of his character. Frequently the abdication is also described as a political crisis, but it was hardly that. Edward was incredibly foolish in this affair, and the cards were all in Baldwin's hands. Nonetheless, it is an important episode in British history, and it turns upon the clearly evolving character of the monarchy in this century. Kings are not as other men.

Edward was not a reproduction, but a badly crafted, amateur-ish, copy of his grandfather Edward VII, "Bertie." David was Bertie writ small. Edward VII would never have considered for a moment giving up the throne for any woman, although he was equally thoughtless and selfish. But the similarities between the men are striking. Each had a genuine public charm, mixed easily with all ranks, and had compassion for human suffering. (Edward VII had made his single speech in the House of Lords, apparently the only address to that chamber by a Prince of Wales, on behalf of public housing, an unfashionable topic in the 1880s.) Edward VIII would have handled Edward VII's famous trip to Paris in 1903 to mend relations with France, an impor-tant step toward the *Entente,* with great aplomb.

Edward met Wallis Warfield Simpson in 1930. At that time she was married to a London stockbroker, Ernest Simpson, her second husband. An American, she had been married briefly, and divorced, in the United States. It is not clear when Edward fell in love with Mrs. Simpson, but certainly by 1934 he had given up all other women, of whom there were several.

One cannot tell what Baldwin knew, or thought, when Edward VIII became King. The official documents on the ab-dication are closed for 100 years (as opposed to thirty for less important matters such as wars). However Prime Ministers are, or were then, in an excellent position to acquire privileged information. In any case, in January 1936, when Edward became King, Mrs. Simpson was the only woman in his life and one must assume that Baldwin was aware of this fact. But it is important that at that time Edward's determination to marry the Ameri-can woman was not clear. As a royal mistress, she was not a problem; there had been many. But if Mrs. Simpson were to be Queen there arose a variety of political, not to say constitutional, problems. At what point the Prime Minister understood this is uncertain, but these considerations defined his position on the affair. Edward's affection for Mrs. Simpson was not by itself dangerous. Even appearing with her in foreign newspaper photographs, if unseemly, was no more than his grandfather had done with Alice Keppel, and Edward was himself single. Only a marriage would bring constitutional danger, and this Baldwin would have to prevent. Meanwhile, as always, he waited upon events. He did not communicate his fears to the King during the first nine months of 1936.

Baldwin's wait ended in October 1936 when Mrs. Simpson began a court action to divorce her husband. Baldwin now had to move, and on October 20 at Edward's private residence, Fort Belvedere, he spoke to the King. What passed between the two men is not entirely coherent, partly because there are so many second- and third-hand accounts. But the burden would seem to be, in a descending level of certainty, that Baldwin asked the King to stop the divorce, told him that he could not marry Mrs. Simpson, and warned that if he did he could not remain King. A twice-divorced American woman could not be Queen of England. However, in the first interview with Baldwin Edward was less than candid. He denied that Mrs. Simpson was more than a friend, and he certainly did not admit that he intended to marry her.

Nevertheless, on October 20, Baldwin had outlined the position that he would hold during the remainder of the affair, that is until December when the King abdicated. While there is really no solid evidence that he believed that Edward was unfit for the throne, Baldwin was perfectly sure that British public opinion, which when he first spoke to the King had had no opportunity for expression because newspapers had not discussed the affair, would never sanction Wallis Warfield Simpson as Queen. He certainly knew that in Europe, most Dominions, and the United States, where the newspapers were covering the King's travails with eager delight and where as Prince of Wales Edward had been hugely popular, the reservoir of good will had been lost. Edward had little sense of public opinion. He had a reliable sense of occasion. He knew exactly how to adjust to the people before him, whether sailors of the Royal Navy or the select crowd in the Royal Enclosure at Ascot. This was not enough. In his own story of the abdication he upbraids Baldwin for refusing to allow him to take his case to the British people, who, apparently he assumed, supported him.

The public phase of the King's great affair was short and final. On October 27 Mrs. Simpson received a decree *nisi* of divorce.

This would allow her to marry six months later. On November 16 Baldwin saw the King again. Edward had by this time come to understand the constitutional arguments Baldwin had tried to make previously. As King his wife became Queen. The Queen was a constitutional figure, in effect public property, not simply a mother of future kings. It followed that the opinions of the British people expressed by the composition of the House of Commons and the resulting government had to be respected.

After this delineation of an English Queen's legal position, for a few days at the end of November 1936 there appeared a proposal by Edward that he marry Mrs. Simpson morganatically. She would give up the dignity of Queen and any children should not be heirs to the throne. Baldwin never seriously considered this proposal saying that it was unknown in English law and would therefore require legislation that neither Parliament, nor the Cabinet, nor he himself, could approve. But he used the occasion to request formally the advice of the Dominions and India, testing his belief that public opinion in the Empire as well as in Great Britain opposed the marriage. With varying degrees of ambiguity all of the Dominions except New Zealand opposed it. He discussed the matter also at some length with Clement Attlee, who since its 1935 defeat had been leader of the Labour party. Attlee made a characteristically sensible point that may have carried some weight with Baldwin. The people of the Dominions, he observed, were more likely to reflect the views of the provinces than of London. The government generally was prone to believe that the sentiments of London's West End were those of the whole country. His own party, said Attlee, "with the exception of a few of the intelligentsia, who could be trusted to take the wrong view on any topic" were in agreement about the unsuitability of Mrs. Simpson. Attlee had already stated firmly that he would decline to form a government should Baldwin resign because of the King's intransigence. Thus the constitutional line around the Monarch now was complete, the trenches manned, the guns in place. If he fought he would be overwhelmed. He could only surrender. In the event he chose to surrender and flee.

Several historians have remarked, quite correctly, that Edward's fate had been decided before the general public— although emphatically not the continually intrusive London social-political world—had become aware there was anything to settle. Despite questions in the House of Commons, answered by ministers in statements that were only a few adjectival phrases short of being falsehoods and with the outright censorship of the incoming world press, British newspapers and the British Broadcasting Corporation, the upper class, in a massive display of solidarity, had maintained silence. All this would not happen today. One has to believe that such forbearance affected the King. Such discretion, he could reflect, meant sympathy and support that the Prime Minister refused to allow him to exploit. Edward said as much in his memoirs. But it could also manifest the selfjustification common in explanations recorded long after the event.

The silence could not last. The attack on Edward began in the afternoon political papers on December 2, prompted by an inconsequential, and misunderstood, speech by the Bishop of Bradford on the King's need for grace, and was taken up in earnest by the metropolitan papers the next day. The King, according to the excellent biography by Frances Donaldson, was horrified. He did not like the British press—probably most monarchs do not—but so far as there was an authentic voice of the nation in 1936, it came from the press. In the trough of Edward's depression, on December 2 after a Cabinet meeting, Baldwin visited him and presented the ultimatum already settled upon: he could not, in any way, morganatically or otherwise, marry Mrs. Simpson and remain King. He must give her up or abdicate. Baldwin hoped sincerely, he affirmed, that the King's choice would be the former. There was no more to be said.

Eight days later on December 10, after more fruitless talk, Edward VIII "by the Grace of God . . . King" signed the Instrument of Abdication and the next day, December 11, in a moving speech to the entire world, echoing indeed the words of the Instrument, he explained that he could not carry the burden of his office "without the help and support of the woman I love." He concluded appropriately with a rousing "God Save the [new] King." Nothing in his kingship, it may be paraphrased, so became him as his manner of leaving it.

Baldwin again had accomplished a political miracle. In 1926 the General Strike had lasted nine days, the public portion of the abdication eight. The new King, previously the Duke of York, happily married with two charming daughters, was duly crowned as George VI on May 12, 1937, the day that had been selected for Edward's coronation. Baldwin resigned two weeks and two days later on May 28 in a bonfire of popularity and genuine love. He was clearly Baldwin the peacemaker. He was succeeded on the same day by Neville Chamberlain, "inevitably," as Chamberlain himself wrote that evening. Edward became His Royal Highness the Duke of Windsor on the day after his abdication. However, when Edward and Mrs. Simpson married on June 3, 1937, King George VI withheld from the new Duchess the title of Her Royal Highness, apparently urged to do so by Baldwin. Edward resented this for the rest of his life. He could not be a morganatic king, but he was, in effect, a morganatic former king.

6 / APPEASEMENT

Historically the abdication of 1936 was a trivial, if widely noticed, affair. It deflected events hardly at all, except to exalt the reputation of Baldwin and simultaneously to provide Winston Churchill with yet another opportunity to display his dependable misapprehension of the realities of politics. Although Churchill's biographer, Martin Gilbert, dismisses its importance, Churchill's intervention on behalf of the King in the last week before the abdication, after Baldwin had delivered his ultimatum, strongly reinforced the already existing contempt for his judgment. Pleading for delay, on December 7 Churchill was howled down in the House of Commons. By this time everyone but he wanted the matter closed, including, it is clear, the King himself.

The diminution of the stature of Winston Churchill, then, must be counted a factor in Britain's slow response to the menace of a revived and rearmed Germany headed by a man who proclaimed the hegemony, not exactly of Germany, but of Germans over Europe, if not the world. Churchill was by no means the only man to call attention to the rising threat across the North Sea, a fact sometimes forgotten, but until 1937, when he was joined by Anthony Eden, he was the only senior Member of Parliament to do so. Moreover he was a senior Privy Counsellor and thus to be called whenever he rose to speak in the House of Commons.

With great reluctance, German President Paul von Hindenburg had appointed Adolf Hitler Chancellor of Germany on January 30, 1933. Hitler was brought to power by the same world economic chaos that had destroyed the Labour government of Ramsay MacDonald a year and a half earlier. In Britain little was known of Hitler the man or of the National Socialist German Workers' Party (the Nazis), although the attacks on Jewish businesses by the party militia, the S.A. (*sturmabteilung*), were well reported in the newspapers and picture magazines. As recently as 1927 the Nazis had held only twelve seats in a Reichstag of 500 and were simply one of many radical fringe groups of the left and right. By the autumn of 1932 the Nazi delegation, always attending the Reichstag in uniform, was well over 200 and decently close to an absolute majority.

To this day German historians have had difficulty coming to terms with, let alone explaining, the fact that Hitler's accession to power was absolutely constitutional. In 1933, his party controlled more seats in the Reichstag than had any Chancellor's party in the short, troubled, history of the German republic. Therefore insofar as they expressed their preferences by vote in a free election, Hitler represented the will of the German people. This would be important for the future. Nazism was indeed a revolutionary creed, but the party's original claim to office, even without an absolute majority, was perfectly legitimate.

British observers were unsure of what to think of the new German leader. Churchill himself admits in his history of the Second World War that he saw Hitler at first chiefly as a super patriot, a point of view with which he could hardly quarrel. The British press looked upon him generally as a puppet of German conservatives, useful to them as a weapon against the Communists.

Among newspaper editors and the middle class public, in the years ahead Hitler's dependable anticommunism became a significant feature in the popular support of Britain's foreign policy of accommodation. The misconception continued even after the so-called "Blood Purge" of June 30, 1934, in which the world watched the murder of several thousand leaders of the S.A. along with a number of other political figures who had taken Hitler's professed anticapitalism too seriously. All of this was conducted with almost boastful publicity. But still Germany was not perceived as a threat to the west. Hitler was, to be sure, a bloodthirsty tyrant and an antisemite, but he was a danger only to the Soviet Union, which he continually proclaimed was his chief enemy. Indeed most, not all, of the strongly nationalist and conservative regimes to Germany's east and southeast, themselves threatened by Soviet intrigue, welcomed the assertive new Germany. In January 1934 Poland signed a nonaggression treaty with its neighbor.

Hence Nazi anticommunism became a prime constituent of Britain's policy of "appeasement" (of Hitler and Germany). How many voters allowed it to determine their behavior in the voting booth is unknown. Nor can polling organizations explain why voters provide a given response to an opinion pollster before an election and contradict it a few days later in their vote. But for the historian it is a conundrum that he must attempt to answer. Should he be wrong his colleagues will inform him soon enough. However, for a government leader to make a mistake in interpreting the public mood is political suicide, as the careers of both Stanley Baldwin and Neville Chamberlain demonstrated. In the midst of the bombing of Britain in 1940, Baldwin, who had been the most beloved man in Britain when he retired in 1937, reflected aloud that the iron gates of his seat, Astley Hall, scheduled to be removed for the war effort, should be left standing: he might need them against angry mobs. "They hate me so," he murmured sadly. Chamberlain has suffered similarly but mercifully after his death. The umbrella and the fluttering paper he proudly waved to the newsreel cameras at Heston airport when he returned from Munich on October 1, 1938, have become symbols of pusillanimity in office.

Baldwin and Chamberlain, ever identified with the dreaded word "appeasement," were neither stupid nor unpatriotic, nor, for that matter, were they ill-informed. The problem for the historian and, no less, for the informed citizen of the western world ever since must be: How did it happen? How could Baldwin and, more visibly, Chamberlain, have been so wrong? The matter is of more than academic importance. Since the Second World War the policy of the western democracies has been the opposite of appeasement: to meet force with force. Hundreds of billions of dollars have been spent and hundreds of thousands of lives lost in pursuit of deterrence, now termed containment.

This has become for us the legacy of the 1930s: that authoritarian, revolutionary, and expansionist regimes must be resisted, by force if necessary, anywhere in the world. Such, of course, had been Britain's policy for two centuries before World War

II. With a worldwide Empire, it had worldwide interests. Why, one wonders, in this one instance, was there such excessive tenderness for Adolf Hitler? Two factors have already been noted: Nazi anticommunism and British ignorance about what, besides the pursuit of anticommunism and antisemitism, Hitler intended to do. He was, after all, hugely popular. In the German elections of 1932 the issues had centered upon problems of the depression, the threat of German communism, and above all on the Nazi demand for revision of the treaty of Versailles.

The Versailles treaty must be accorded major importance in the examination of the roots of appeasement. If Hitler's rantings in 1932 had any ethical foundations at all, they derived from the treaty. There were many in Britain, among them Neville Chamberlain, Lloyd George, and in fact Churchill, who felt Germany had been treated unjustly at the Paris peace conference. Its military forces had been reduced to token size in the expectation that the Allied powers would similarly disarm, which France had consistently refused to do. On the contrary, France had invaded Germany in 1923. Again, Germany had been deprived of territory inhabited by its citizens in contravention of the principle of selfdetermination to which, however, great homage was paid in regard to everyone else. All of this had been done in deference to French demands for military security. And through most of the 1920s that nation had fought to keep Germany in diplomatic limbo. Accordingly, in addition to disgust with the Versailles treaty, there was in British appeasement an ingredient of old-fashioned, Anglo-Saxon, Francophobia. If France felt threatened by Hitler let it take action, many Englishmen agreed. This was clearly a widespread sentiment in 1936 at the time of the German military occupation of the Rhineland (that part of Germany that lay west of the Rhine River). France had devoted the previous fifteen years to the isolation and humiliation of Germany. France should not expect Britain to rescue it again.

Above all there lay like a dead hand, memories of the First World War. Britain had suffered 750,000 men killed in action and more than twice that number wounded. Every village had its cenotaph inscribed with the names of the fallen "for King and Country." A number of distinguished families whose names had been exalted in wars against France in the eighteenth century disappeared in the wars against the Germans in the twentieth. Not a son survived.

There may be no way to evaluate the simple antiwar sentiment of the 1930s except to say that it was clear, palpable, and important. It was expressed in some cases as a philosophical pacifism among intellectuals, a brotherhood-of-man ideology, often associated with doctrinal socialism. To many more it was a simple fear of violence, of being killed. Much of this proceeded from the unknown but easily imagined horror of massive aerial bombardment of Britain's crowded cities. There would be huge civilian casualties, and worse, widespread civilian panic. Let it be emphasized quickly that these grave anticipations were not simply the whinings of a few hysterical cowards. The Cabinet and the military leaders took the danger of heavy bombing very seriously indeed. The World War I precedents had not been forgotten.

The First World War provided the lessons. In the spring of 1917 the Germans began seriously to replace their airships (Zeppelins) with the new multiengine Gotha bomber, the prototype of the bombardment family of aircraft still in existence. Although the Germans never succeeded in putting more than twenty-two airplanes over London at one time, raids on June 13, 1917 when 104 people were killed and on July 7 with forty-six more, resulted in public panic and outrage which the government could not ignore. One result, as has been noted, was the creation of the Royal Air Force. (These two raids caused about one-tenth of the total civilian dead from air raids in all of Britain during World War I, 1,413 dead plus 3,407 wounded.)

The conclusion drawn by British, as well as European and American, defense planners was that airplanes were the weapons of the future. This thinking was codified by the Italian air officer, General Giulio Douhet, early in the 1920s in an essay arguing that aircraft alone, by mass bombing and gassing of cities, would so demoralize the civilian population that the government would have no option but to surrender. Military victories on the ground would be irrelevant and unnecessary.

The grim "Douhet thesis" became generally accepted doctrine even though most people could not have identified it. Long-range bombing capability was the measure of a nation's strength. There would be no stopping the airplanes. "The bomber will always get through," predicted Baldwin. The only defense was the possession of an equally potent bombardment air fleet, in effect deterrence. The sense of imagined horror was increased by the assumption, which again the government shared, that the enemy would use poison gas in addition to high explosive and incendiary bombs. (In 1938 the government began the distribution of gas masks to the entire population, including respirator equipment for infants' perambulators. It was to be carried at all times. The fine for being without it was five shillings.) The public was hardly reassured by the release in 1937 of a film "The Shape of Things to Come," from a 1933 novel by H. G. Wells, which featured terrifyingly realistic bombing raids upon London that caused great slaughter and widespread hysteria.

The core of the debate over British defense policy, the inevitable counterpart of the debate over the foreign policy of appeasement, turned upon the size of the German air force, the *Luftwaffe*, in comparison to the size of the Royal Air Force, the R.A.F. If the Germans gained air superiority the destruction of Britain was assured. A very large segment of the population— whether a majority or not is impossible to say—concluded simply that war was impossible. Peace, in effect, was worth any price. The arguments have been recited: Hitler's anticommunism, the injustice of the Treaty of Versailles, the distaste for France's indifference to anyone's interests but its own. All of these coalesced with doctrinal pacifism in the conviction that Hitler had to be excused. Detestable as he was, his claims would have to be conceded.

Yet still there was more to be considered. Others held that Hitler was not as bad as he seemed to be. The New Germany was open, clearly prosperous, and content, while building construction was everywhere, and the unemployed had disappeared. Britons were invited to visit Germany and to go wherever they liked, the opposite of the Soviet Union. These were achievements that Britain, with 2,000,000 unemployed, could hardly disparage. In 1936 Germany provided the site for the Olympic Games. They were a huge success except for Hitler's bad manners toward a black runner from Columbus, Ohio, Jesse Owens, who won three gold medals in track and field events.

In any case, the alternative was too horrible to contemplate. Germany was the wrong enemy; its goals were in the East and did not concern Britain. To risk destruction from the skies in order to make war upon Germany because of its demands in eastern Europe simply was not to be countenanced. Neville Chamberlain put this view succinctly in a speech on September 27, 1938. At Godesburg on September 22 he had rejected Hitler's demands for an immediate and essentially unconditional cession of the Czech Sudetenland (that part of Czechoslovakia bordering on Germany and Austria). On September 26 Hitler demanded Czech withdrawal from the Sudetenland within two days, or war. The next day on the BBC, Chamberlain defined the nation's ghastly choices precisely: national destruction or capitulation. "How horrible, fantastic, incredible, it is that we should be digging slit trenches and trying on gas masks here because of a quarrel in a far-away country between people of whom we know nothing." In contests between imagined disaster and reasoned action, imagined disaster will win every time. Two days later Chamberlain flew to Munich to concede Hitler's demands. When he returned he was cheered to the skies. He received a reported 10,000 telegrams thanking him for saving the peace. He was invited to Buckingham Palace to appear on the balcony with the King and Queen before a rapturous crowd of tens of thousands. From a window in Downing Street he announced that at Munich he had achieved "peace with honour. I believe it is peace for our time." Precisely eleven months and three days later Britain went to war with Germany.

CHAMBERLAIN AND FOREIGN POLICY

Pacifism trapped British politicians as in a vise. One jaw pressed them with a clear, if undefined, sense of what they could not do. The other exerted pressure to do what they knew they must not. Baldwin, who counts as the founder of the appeasement policy, made this dilemma clear. On November 12, 1936 he referred to a by-election in London's East Fulham borough three years before on October 25, 1933, nine months after Hitler had taken power. The Conservative candidate had strongly supported rearmament. He had been heavily defeated by a pacifist Labour candidate in a borough that, with boundary changes, had remained staunchly Conservative since 1885. East Fulham has received much scholarly attention: it was a three-cornered race, and so on. But its importance lies not in its political details but in its effect upon Stanley Baldwin. Three years later, after Germany had announced military conscription and the existence of an air force, after the reoccupation of the Rhineland and after the outbreak of the Spanish Civil War, Baldwin explained its lesson to the House of Commons. Why had he not made rearmament an issue in the election of November 1935? He referred to the example of East Fulham and continued: "I put my views before the House with appalling frankness . . . supposing I had gone to the country and . . . said that we must rearm, does anybody think that this pacific democracy would have rallied to that cry? I cannot think of anything that would have made the loss of the election from my point of view more certain." Invariably, historians have used this statement as an illustration of the flawed character of Stanley Baldwin who was more concerned with winning elections than with defending the nation. This is unfair even though Baldwin took elections very seriously indeed. The dilemma he described was real and one that touches the core of democratic politics: should an elected political leader take the actions that his access to secret information and his own reason tells him are necessary even though he knows they will be repugnant to the bulk of the voters who put him in office, or should he do what he believes the voters want? When the two differ, should he respond to his own best judgment or to the will of the majority? Certainly every democratic idealist would say he should consult his judgment, but it is equally certain that disregarding for any length of time the wishes of the electorate in a democracy hardly guarantees a prosperous career in politics. But far worse, even with the sacrifice of his political life, a man does not ensure the success of his policy. This was Baldwin's point in November 1936. Hitler was rearming, not secretly; he was doing so openly and proudly. As Baldwin spoke, visitors to Germany were being invited to the trials of a newly designed fighter, the Messerschmitt Bf109, which in the next year would break the world speed record, a fact announced with great fanfare. Had the Labour party with George Lansbury as leader won the November 1935 election, chances of rebuilding Britain's defenses would have disappeared. Money, Labour insisted, should be spent on the poor, not weapons. Politically it made no sense to raise the issue of rearmament if one really cared about strengthening Britain. Was it not better from Baldwin's and the Conservatives' point of view to remain in office, soldier on, and do what could be done?

The democratic political leader, faced with an electorate hostile to a decision that he knows must be taken, is helpless. This may be true especially in the area of foreign policy where issues are complex, public knowledge slight, and failure catastrophic. As another example within the purview of this essay, one may cite Lloyd George's perplexity at Paris over the treatment of Germany. He had not gone to Paris with the intention of punishing Germany. He had called what he expected to be a wartime election in part to avoid having to discuss a settlement with Germany. Even after the Armistice he had resisted discussing foreign affairs until the last few days before the poll and concentrated instead upon reconstruction, which he described as making Britain a land fit for heroes to live in. Then, as war prisoners began to return, public attention turned to Germany and could not be deflected. Inevitably the slogan of a land fit for heroes was replaced by "make Germany pay." On December 14, 1918, the electorate, in what could fairly be described as a frenzy of revengefulness, voted for punishment of Germany. Lloyd George found himself under orders to make a punitive treaty. With the French insistence upon large payments for themselves and with a majority of Conservative MPs in Britain reminding him of their electoral pledges, he had no avenue of escape.

Eighteen years later, between 1937 and 1939, Neville Chamberlain's freedom of initiative was similarly bound, even though he unmistakably concurred with the public's opinion. In the critical last two weeks of September 1938, during which he had visited Germany three times, Chamberlain's conversations with the Cabinet demonstrated that selfdetermination for the Sudeten Germans, to which Hitler continually referred, had been for him a convincing argument. Britain could not go to war against selfdetermination. Yet second, Chamberlain was personally determined to refrain from any threat of war at all, and the Cabinet agreed that the country would never approve such a threat. Nor, for that matter, were the army and the air force comfortable with any proposal for the coercion of Germany.

Chamberlain simply could not have enforced military sanctions on Germany at the time of the Munich meeting of 1938. Neither popular support nor military power was available. But again, he never intended to do so. He did not care, as he had told Hitler on September 15 at Berchtesgaden, whether the Sudeten Germans were inside or outside the Reich. He believed—it cannot be said too many times—that Hitler had a good case. Millions of other Britons agreed.

A defense of Chamberlain, made repeatedly since 1938, has held that the Munich settlement, however cruel to Czechoslovakia, was really only a tactic of delay. Britain needed time to rearm. The enthusiasts of this argument have insisted that the eleven months gained between Munich and the outbreak of war enabled Britain to survive. This point of view ignores the fact that Germany also had eleven more months and used it more effectively. Further, in its two invasions of Czechoslovakia on October 1, 1938 and March 15, 1939, Germany acquired not only some 500 modern and well-made Czech tanks but the vast Skoda armament works at Pilsen in Bohemia. The same invasions deprived the British and French of the support of nearly thirty well-equipped Czech divisions, a much larger force than the British army at that time.

More revealing in terms of British policy and the character of Neville Chamberlain, however, is the Prime Minister's refusal in the months after Munich, actually until March 1939, to permit any increase in British weapons procurement. Indeed, on October 31, 1938, he told the Cabinet that he looked forward to decreasing soon the rate of rearmament. Chamberlain, as perhaps has been overemphasized in this essay, believed with complete honesty and total misapprehension that he had resolved the problem of Nazi expansion. Hitler had said he had no interest in the remaining part of Czechoslovakia. He wanted only to unite Germans. "We do not want Czechs in the Reich." Later he had assured Chamberlain that the Sudetenland was the "end of his territorial claims in Europe."

Obviously Chamberlain accepted these assurances. After hard bargaining, he had made a contract, which he was sure had saved the peace of Europe. He had conducted negotiations and had a piece of paper upon which the agreement was written. This was the English way of doing business. In this case, Chamberlain's objective was European peace. Hitler had said his goal was the same except that he was bound also to champion the rights of Germans living in other countries. If these Germans wished to join the Reich, as they clearly did, who was he, Chamberlain, to say they could not? But Hitler was interested only in Germans. He would stop with the Sudetenland. Thus, to Chamberlain, peace, the overriding objective, was worth the sacrifice of Czech integrity. Both Europe and the remaining, non-German, part of Czechoslovakia would be better off in the long run. Had Chamberlain been dealing with the British Medical Association as Minister of Health or the Bank of England when at the Treasury, such businesslike reasoning would have made sense. But Hitler was a man beyond his experience, guided by a *daemon* which he identified as the general will of the German people that was communicated solely to him. Even were it explained, Chamberlain would not have understood.

The Munich settlement was the quintessence of appeasement. It differed from all that Britain had ever allowed before. After it the unstoppable slide toward war began. The Munich agreement had no diplomatic sanction such as that which partially excused the German occupation of the Rhineland and of Austria. The former was, after all, German territory while Austria had petitioned twice in the years after the war to be allowed to join Germany. The nation's welcome to the German army in March 1938, widely reported, testified to its validity. In any case, Hitler's violations were only breaches of the already discredited treaty of Versailles. But the German seizure of the Sudetenland, agreed to by Britain, involved the dismemberment of a non-German, democratic state whose integrity France, if not Britain, was obligated to protect. Its boundaries were those long established under the old Austro-Hungarian Empire, not the result of dubious negotiations at Paris. Czechoslovakia had been prepared to defend itself and was abandoned by its allies. It appeared that Czechoslovakia had been sacrificed by Britain and France in order to save themselves.

The dismemberment of Czechoslovakia would be regarded differently today had it in fact saved the peace, but it did not. It could not have done so. As is now known, Hitler had already determined upon expansion to the East and Southeast even at the risk of war, which for economic reasons had to begin before 1942, and Czechoslovakian financial and industrial resources were by far the most valuable in Eastern Europe. Within six months he had seized the rest of that unhappy country.

Czechoslovakia had descended into chaos after Munich. President Edward Beneš, one of the republic's founders, resigned and left the country. A Slovakian separatist movement developed. Hitler simply took advantage of this disorder, some of which Germany helped to sponsor, to move troops into the remainder of the nation on March 15, 1939. There was no diplomatic ceremony, no ultimatum, no explanation except that authority in Czechoslovakia had collapsed. The Czechs could accept occupation or risk war. It was an act of contempt for the West and for Hitler's own promises.

On Friday, March 17, Chamberlain pronounced the end of appeasement in a speech in Birmingham broadcast to the nation. It was the statement conveying less outrage at a broken international agreement than personal insult. Hitler had lied to him, had broken his word. What had become he asked, with something near to rage or misery in his voice, of the assurance: "We do not want Czechs in the Reich?" Chamberlain had been not only defeated but dishonored.

The results of his announcement came swiftly. On March 31, stimulated by rumors, only half true, Chamberlain announced a unilateral guarantee of Poland. Should Germany attack Poland "His Majesty's Government would feel themselves bound at once to lend the Polish Government all the support in their power." In the next few weeks, the army, the neglected service that at the end of 1938 could promise only two divisions ready for overseas operations, was ordered to prepare plans for expansion to thirty-two divisions. Most uncharacteristic of Cham-

berlain, and demonstrating best what he felt had occurred, was
the enactment in May of six months of military training for all
men at age twenty. This was not quite universal military conscription, although the newspapers treated it as if it were. Nonetheless,
it was unprecedented in peacetime in British history.

More privately, government departments were ordered to
prepare for the dispersal of their records, the National Gallery
of its pictures. As a chilling illustration of what sort of war the
government expected, orders were placed for 1,000,000 papier-
mâché coffins and 3,000,000 printed death certificates. The
historian is compelled to believe that the government—and this
means essentially Chamberlain himself who dominated the
Cabinet completely—had moved in a fortnight from a conviction
that peace at last was at hand to a resignation that war was inevitable. The question was no longer whether Britain would have
to fight, but when.

In view of what happened five months later this statement may
appear to be selfevident to the point of redundancy. But in fact
a number of scholars argue that appeasement continued until
the war began. They point to attempts to compromise with Hitler
and to the tardiness of the British ultimatum that was sent a full
forty-eight hours after Germany invaded Poland. One can only
answer that a feeling that war will surely come does not preclude
attempts to avoid it. In 1914 the British ultimatum expired more
than two days after the German ultimatum to Belgium.

However, the best evidence in support of the assertion that
Chamberlain had given up any hope of peace lies in the comparison of the frantic scramble to build the armed forces in the
too few months remaining with the measured coolness, almost
indifference, that had been shown toward similar activities in
the previous years. Hitherto British military preparations had
been entirely defensive. The navy received a decent number of
new ships and many more were under construction. Substantial sums had been spent on fighter aircraft design and construction, just enough as it turned out. At the same time, as is now
known, the government pushed vigorously the development of
radio detection and ranging (radar).

On the other hand, the army was, if anything, in worse shape
in 1939 than it had been a decade earlier. Unbelievably, until
the first months of 1939 the Cabinet had been unable to bring

itself to make a decision upon whether a military force should go to the continent at all. There was no treaty with France nor even an understanding.

Britain had no plans beyond a naval blockade in case of war with Germany. What the French command intended to do should the Germans remain on the defensive in the West was unclear. In the event French forces did nothing, and therein lies the story of the first seven months of the war. Far worse, diplomatic obligation and military capability were clumsily out of step, as they had been in 1914. On March 31, Chamberlain, apparently without much reflection and on what seems to have been little more than unconfirmed reports of a German move toward Poland or Romania, had given his unilateral open-ended pledge of protection to Poland. But how would this be honored? The question came up immediately. In what way, he was immediately asked in the House of Commons, did he propose to help defend Poland? He was reminded that in the debates over Munich he had argued that a settlement was necessary because no way existed to convey relieving forces into Czechoslovakia. But similarly, it was pointed out, not one British soldier would be available to Poland, yet its security had been guaranteed.

The only nation able to come effectively to Poland's aid was the Soviet Union. But here lay another complication proceeding from the impromptu nature of Chamberlain's declaration. The guarantee to Poland had been made without the negotiation of any reciprocal promises. The Soviet Union professed, perhaps untruthfully, to be willing to enter a four-power alliance against Germany. The difficulty was that Poland firmly refused to enter into any sort of an agreement with the Soviet Union, thus excluding the only power that could realistically help it against the Nazis. Despite Polish intransigence, the British, far too late, sent a diplomatic mission, the "Strang mission," to Moscow to seek a way of bringing the Soviets into the Western security system. It arrived on August 11, 1939.

Eleven days after the British delegation arrived in Moscow and before it had been able to see any responsible officials, on the plea that it was duck-shooting season and no one was in the city, its purpose was crushed. On August 22 the Russians announced that the German foreign minster, Joachim von

Ribbentrop, was flying to Moscow and that the two nations would sign a pact. On the following day the world was treated to newsreel pictures of von Ribbentrop and Vyacheslav Molotov, the Soviet foreign minister, signing a treaty of friendship with Joseph Stalin smiling benignly in the background.

The treaty was Ribbentrop's creation and it ensured a Polish war. Moreover, it gave the Soviet Union a good deal more than friendship. It purchased Soviet neutrality by the concession to the Soviets of the Baltic republics and of an approximately 100-mile-strip of eastern Poland. Ribbentrop promised Hitler that it would bring another Western capitulation. Despite Chamberlain's guarantees and Poland's long-standing alliance with France, Poland would fight alone. Mistakenly regarding the British as cool-headed and rational, Ribbentrop and Hitler assumed that no British government would commit the fortunes of the nation to so foolhardy a venture as the defense of Poland without the cooperation of the Soviet Union.

The German threat to Poland was relatively new. Chamberlain does not appear to have heard anything concrete about a breakdown in relations between the two states until a few days before he made his guarantee on March 31, although rumors of trouble had been circulating since the beginning of the year 1939. Until the fall of 1938, relations between Germany and Poland had been relatively easy. There were bonds of sympathy. Poland had a large Jewish population, a strain of antisemitism in its culture, and both nations perceived the Soviet Union as an enemy. But western Poland contained also a substantial German population and that portion between East Prussia and the rest of Germany which the Germans called West Prussia (the so-called Polish corridor), as well as the Free City of Danzig, were heavily German in population. The latter, administered by the League of Nations, had been part of the old Hanseatic League and in 1939 was home to a large and pugnacious Nazi party.

Hitler was enraged at Chamberlain's assurance of support to Poland. He seems to have regarded it as an interference in German affairs. Within a month he had given orders for the planning of a military operation against Poland and had determined to attack at the first opportunity. The only problem remaining was the settlement with the Soviet Union. Approaches began in April. When the Soviet obstacle was removed in August, the war began immediately. Hitler never sought and indeed avoided direct negotiations with Poland.

German armed forces attacked Poland at dawn on September 1. Britain delayed until September 3 before sending an ultimatum to Germany, but its deadline was only two hours after delivery of the note and the Cabinet had decided upon war the evening before, in effect eighteen hours after the commencement of hostilities. At 11:15 a.m. on September 3 Chamberlain told the nation over the BBC that the Second German War had begun. Immediately after the speech an air raid alert sounded in London, but it turned out to be a false alarm.

According to Hitler's interpreter, Paul Schmidt, his master received the ultimatum calmly, although he shot an accusing glance at Ribbentrop who was looking glumly out of the window of Hitler's Reichschancellery office. When Schmidt left the Fuhrer's office the anteroom was crowded with high-ranking officers who demanded to know what had happened. After Schmidt explained, he heard Hermann Göering, Hitler's first lieutenant and commander of the German Air Force mutter, "If we lose this one, may God have mercy on us."

A few comparisons with the events preceding the first war may be appropriate at this point. In both 1914 and 1939 British politicians allowed their nation to assume military obligations for which the armed forces were quite unprepared. But this parallel should not be pushed too far. The declaration of war in 1914 was an act foreseen at least since 1911 and was based upon a policy of informal commitment to France, the *Entente*, that was nearly a decade old. If Britain's army was inadequate for the task assigned to it, the responsibility lay in the universal ignorance of the realities of modern war. In theory the army was well-prepared, newly rearmed and professionalized, with six full strength divisions prepared to go abroad at a moment's notice. Britain's military leaders, as well as the population at large, had been confident and enthusiastic.

In 1939 almost every condition and assumption contradicted the previous experience. The military leaders both in Britain and France were most uncomfortable with the sudden turn toward war in the spring of 1939. The logic of appeasement had lain in the conviction that Germany had been unfairly treated at Versailles, many of Hitler's demands thus were justified, and that with modern weapons war was unthinkable. In Britain there was moderate spending upon defense but there was no real rearmament, and the army got nothing. Then in March of 1939 everything changed. A military force and even a policy for its use had suddenly to be improvised. The result was a war for which the nation was neither militarily nor emotionally prepared, begun on most unfavorable terms for Britain, and one that it could not have won with the resources available at the time of its declaration. In March 1939, in a rare moment of rashness, in anger and with little consultation, Chamberlain had given a blank check to Poland, and so had put his nation in a position to be forced into war. The initiative, which had been Britain's in 1914, was given to Germany in 1939.

7 / THE WAR, 1939

THE FIRST PHASE: WAR WITHOUT FIGHTING

September 1939–April 1940

Like the first war, the second is easily divided into phases which can be entitled and defined. The first, lasting from Britain and France's declarations of hostilities on September 3, 1939 to April 9, 1940 when Germany attacked Denmark and Norway, is usually ridiculed as "the Phony War" the "Sitzkrieg," or the "Bore War." If rather inelegant, these titles are perfectly valid. Legally Britain and France were at war with Germany, but except at sea and for fewer than four weeks in Poland, there was no combat. The British hurried four ill-equipped divisions to France and promised six more by February 1940. But the Allied forces commander, French General Maurice Gamelin, his grand strategy conditioned by the existence of massive and complex fixed fortifications on the Franco-German frontier, the Maginot Line, made no move to attack into southern Germany. Poland was left to die alone. On September 27 Warsaw radio, broadcasting continuously Chopin's *Marche Militaire*, went off the air.

After the surrender of Poland and before the German attack on Denmark and Norway five months and twelve days later, the central theme of British history in the second war is not military. Abroad the army was doing nothing, although gaining valuable time for equipping and training. The first British army battle casualty did not occur until two months after the declaration of war. The R.A.F. dropped pamphlets telling the German people, whose army had effortlessly overrun Poland, that they could not win. Only the sea provided a venue for killing. German submarines began unwarned attacks upon British and French shipping and invaded the Scapa Flow naval base to sink a battleship. The tortured problems of limited or unlimited submarine warfare never arose. Britain lost 800,000 tons of shipping in the first nine months, although in December 1939 the navy succeeded in catching and forcing the scuttling of the German "pocket battleship" *Admiral Graf Spee* (in reality a large, 10 to 12,000 ton, armored cruiser with eleven-inch guns). It cheered people up at home and apparently made Hitler angry, but accomplished little more.

The important story during the first five months of the war deals with Britain itself. The measured pace of mobilization of British arms reflected the stubborn reproach, almost a resentment, apparent within the population to the fact of the war's existence. In 1939 there was none of the euphoria that had accompanied the declaration of war in 1914. The mood was somber, resigned, or angry. Chamberlain's radio statement on September 3, as had his speech on September 27, 1938, before Munich, captured exactly the public sentiment: "Everything that I have worked for, everything that I have hoped for, everything that I have believed in during my public life, has crashed into ruins." Leaving out "my public life," anyone in Britain could have said the same. The war was not an adventure nor a joyous crusade. At best it was a grim duty or a defeat, at worst a disaster. Harold Nicolson, MP and his wife, Vita Sackville-West, provided themselves with poison to prepare for a prudent suicide. Captain B. H. Liddell Hart, military correspondent of *The Times*, a tactical scholar and historian who probably knew as much about the British army as any civilian alive, with the possible exception of J. F. C. Fuller, resigned from the newspaper and retired in misery to his country cottage. As it stood, he knew, the Allies mathematically could not win. The numbers simply did not add up. He was, of course, correct.

It follows that the ordinary, badly informed, citizen tried either to forget the war so far as possible or to get away from it. London was emptied of one-and-a-third million tearful school children in anticipation of bombing. These plans, long prepared, were like nearly all other government preparations essentially defensive. The children were to go to the west where "billeting officers" (volunteers from the local gentry) who had powers of compulsion would assign them to homes. The evacuation, organized around schools, was a smooth success, as one would expect from the civil service. The children's reception was far less so. The village professional classes demonstrated English status consciousness at its most egregious, and the cultural disfunctions between the two groups have kept sociologists busy for half a century. On the other hand, as perhaps might have been expected, the less affluent and the older county gentry seem to have made them welcome if not always comfortable. The first evacuation was less than durable and half the children were back at home by Christmas. There had been no bombing of London; hence for many there was no war.

The children's evacuation was accompanied, if not matched in size, by the exodus of adults, many elderly, who prepared reasonably to wait in country hotels for the war to end. Children of the well-to-do were sent to the United States or Canada. The fear of bombing, so frequently referred to here, was very real. This attitude, styled within the government as "The Deep Shelter Mentality," caused some concern to the Cabinet. The poet John Betjeman's ironic little verse catches the feeling:

> Gracious Lord, oh bomb the Germans
> Spare their women for Thy sake
> And if that is not too easy
> We will pardon Thy mistake.
> But Gracious Lord, what ere shall be
> Don't let anyone bomb me.

In all of this search for personal security, the atmosphere was less of panic than of a kind of disengagement. The war was the government's business. The ordinary citizen would do no less than his duty, nor any more. He was saying, "I do not doubt the war will be won, but so far as possible it will be won without me."

Official policy complimented exactly the unhealthy public detachment. There was no emergency. Time was on the side of the Allies. The Royal Navy and the Maginot Line enclosed Hitler in a ring of steel against which he would batter himself to death or else quietly starve. In November 1939 Chamberlain, writing to his sister as he did nearly every day, predicted that the war would be over in the spring of 1940 when Hitler realized that he could not win. Then in the spring of 1940, on April 4, just six days before the Germans attacked Denmark and Norway, he made a much more celebrated public statement, never to be forgotten. "Hitler missed the bus," he asserted, by failing to attack France and Britain six months earlier before they were ready. Now, by implication, they were invulnerable. Until Hitler surrendered, Britain, under Chamberlain's always prudent stewardship, would organize carefully and in measured phases the vast resources of the British Empire and the world. There would be none of the planless distribution of contracts to unknown manufacturers, the enlistment of men for whom there were no uniforms, or the conscription of skilled engineers as riflemen in the trenches, which had occurred in the first war. Chamberlain had spent an unhappy year in 1916–17 attempting to organize a national service for war and was adamant that it should not occur again. In May of 1940, with the war nearly a year old, there were still a half-million registered unemployed. Britain's power would be built according to schedule. Full mobilization would be achieved only in 1942. Meanwhile the slogan was "Business as usual."

At the same time, Chamberlain could reflect, everything that needed to be done had been done. Even before the war, on August 29, Parliament had passed the Emergency Powers (Defence) Act allowing the Cabinet by Orders in Council (i.e., by decree) to convert the nation into a dictatorship. Food rationing, with control of industrial raw materials and (Chamberlain remembering his unhappy experience under Lloyd George) manpower, were immediately instituted. A comprehensive system of air raid wardens enforced the nightly blackouts. Posters appeared everywhere urging citizens to carry gas masks, to be sure no sliver of light appeared in their windows, to keep secrets: "Loose lips sink ships." Merchants taped their shop windows and piled sandbags around doorways. To the visitor from the United States, Britain seemed to be at war. But lacking were a sense of urgency or purpose and a plan to gain victory.

THE SECOND PHASE: NORWAY

Not every member of the British government believed in the expediency of waiting for Hitler to move or that time was irrevocably and forever on the side of the Allies. Among the least complacent was Winston Churchill, whom Chamberlain had recalled to the Admiralty on September 3, 1939. Churchill's reappearance in the government at the Admiralty, in an office highly visible and one of the traditional "glittering prizes," was more than a surprise—it was a shock. In the late thirties, Churchill's career, it was assumed by politicians, was over. In Cabinet he was infantile, rude, overbearing, incapable of compromise, an impossible colleague. He had disgraced himself during Edward VIII's abdication. He could not sustain contradiction. His tantrums were famous. Siegfried Sassoon had called him a "man-child."

Yet as the only man who could control him, David Lloyd George, understood he was a genius. If put to work and pointed in the right direction, he was unstoppable. Thus Lloyd George had brought him back into the government in 1917 at much political cost.

Chamberlain detested Churchill as much as anyone, but with the disciplined sense of reality that had made him Prime Minister he understood Churchill's value. So, as in 1917, Churchill was saved again. It is fair to say that without this invitation Churchill would have disappeared, overlooked like an uncut diamond with incalculable consequences for the story of Britain. As in classical tragedy, the gods had made him fit only for supreme power or execution.

Characteristically Churchill's views of the war disagreed entirely with those of the Cabinet. He was certain Germany would not submit tamely to strangulation. Norway provided the immediate focus of his concern. On November 30, 1939, the Soviet Union attacked Finland. The Finns defended themselves with great courage and for several months with a good deal of success. The western Allies applauded and searched for means to send help. Finland's desperation directed attention to Norway and Sweden. Only through those nations could the brave Finns be reached. Both however refused to allow arms to cross their territory, citing neutrality. Yet in winter when the Gulf of Bothnia was frozen, Norway allowed Germany to use the 2,000 miles of its rugged Atlantic coastline waters to ship iron ore mined in Sweden from the northern port of Narvik to Germany's Baltic ports. From there it went to the steel mills of the Ruhr valley to feed the Nazi war machine. The truth of course was that the

Scandinavian nations were far more afraid of Germany than of the Allies and to appease it were sacrificing their neighbor.

Churchill was furious. Norway and Sweden were neutral only toward the Allies. Since the beginning of the war he had bombarded the Cabinet with memoranda demanding action against the shipments of Swedish iron ore. The Cabinet, in effect Chamberlain, demurred. At the end of November came the Soviet attack on Finland and its stirring but unheeded appeals for aid. On January 20, 1940, on the BBC, Churchill warned "neutral nations"—unspecified, but clear—not to depend upon buying Hitler's good will. "Each one hopes," he stated in undiplomatic language, "that if he feeds the crocodile enough the crocodile will eat him last." Only a little more than two weeks later on February 16, 1940 the German merchant ship *Altmark* attempted to use Norwegian territorial waters to take to Germany several hundred Allied merchant seamen captured by the now sunk *Graf Spee*. The *Altmark* was intercepted within Norwegian waters by a British destroyer and the prisoners were rescued. The Norwegians, who claimed to have inspected the ship, protested a violation of neutral territory, not to Germany but to Britain.

There may have been an intentional inference in Churchill's speech that the British navy as well as the crocodile possessed only limited patience. In any case, after the *Altmark* incident the Cabinet, which had dithered for months over coercion of Norway and aid to Finland, began to plan for a landing at Narvik to seize the railway to Sweden. Only by this route could Finland be reached with the added advantage that in the winter the occupation of the port would interdict German ore shipments. This plan fell apart with the surrender of Finland to the Russians on March 12, 1940. The Cabinet then returned to proposals for mining the Norwegian inland waterways, which was finally carried out by airplanes on the night of April 8–9. At 5:00 A.M. the next morning, German military, naval, and air forces attacked Denmark and Norway.

The German attack upon Norway, an operation demanded by Hitler personally which was completed successfully by June 8, receives limited attention in general histories of the second war, but it is of great interest to military historians. The German command, itself unenthusiastic about the project, broke all of the textbook rules of engagement in this assault. The Germans divided their forces, had no assured means of logistical support, attacked over seas they did not control against numerically superior forces, and depended entirely on surprise in an operation too complex for them to be sure that communication security was complete. One can only say that no one but the Germans would have attempted it.

The key to the attack lay in air power. The Germans were able to seize all Norwegian airfields at the outset and so protect and supply widely dispersed and lightly armed ground forces even as far away as Narvik, a critical point. For Britain, Norway provided the startling lesson that control of the seas meant little without command of the air over them. Certainly, the Royal Navy was able to sink or damage a substantial portion of Hitler's navy and to drown a good many Germany troop reinforcements, but they were unable to supply, without crippling losses in ships, the British military force landed at Narvik. Eventually on June 8, as the German invasion of France drew to an end, the British Narvik force, five times the size of the German, was evacuated.

For the British, there were four lessons here, each one slowly learned but of resounding importance for the years ahead. First, naval vessels, no matter how modern or heavily armed, could not come within the range of land-based bombers without great danger. Second, in Norway Britain came to understand the price of having consolidated the Royal Flying Corps and the Royal Naval Air Service rather than funding a separate air force: British naval aircraft simply could not engage the German Bf109 fighter on equal terms. Third, less clear but perhaps most disturbing, Allied assumptions about the German army, shared both by the government and the press, were incorrect. They had always held that the German soldier was an unwilling conscript, a cryptodemocrat, briefly trained and no match for the dedicated Allied soldier. It followed that the Germans had won in Poland because of overwhelming numbers and superior equipment. This was of course essentially the way German propaganda four years later would characterize the United States army. In Norway this was proved untrue. German forces there fought against great odds. Nevertheless, when the tiny force in Narvik was driven out of the town on May 28 it retreated down the railway toward Sweden, held on with supplies from aircraft, and eventually was victorious. This was a source of perpetual concern to Churchill and may have become a determinant in his strategic thinking in the latter part of the war. In Africa and Sicily he knew the Allies had prevailed. But in battalion actions the German army had won too often.

Finally, in seizing Norway, Hitler gained a coastline that the Allies could not keep secure, nor even under surveillance. Thus for practical purposes Hitler had outflanked the British naval blockade which was supposed to strangle him. Moreover German naval vessels could now be moved from North Sea ports to remote inlets within the fjords, guarded by towering mountains which made them virtually immune to bombing. The Norwegian occupation changed entirely the course of the naval war. During the first war, sweeping German surface vessels from the high seas had been mostly accomplished within the first six months. In the second war, this took four years against a much smaller German fleet. Even then the most serious constraint upon German ship movements in the second war was not the presence of the Royal Navy, but the shortage of oil.

THE CHURCHILL GOVERNMENT

In Britain the extent of the Norwegian disaster was clouded by censorship, but the failure of the government to plan for such an eventuality, manifest in the "missed the bus" speech, was obvious enough. On May 7, 1940, the House of Commons began a debate on the conduct of the Norwegian operations still in progress. Soon it was clear that the House was less concerned with fixing blame for Norway, for which the principal responsibility was Churchill's, than in debating Neville Chamberlain's fitness to continue as Prime Minister. For two days, until May 8, the debate raged. Many observers noted that the sharpest attacks came not from the Labour opposition, whose own record on military preparation before the war could hardly bear scrutiny, but from members of the Prime Minister's own party. Churchill himself defended the Prime Minister loyally as indeed he should have. Recent studies have made clear that British uncertainty about whether Trondheim or Narvik should be the target of the principal effort proceeded from Churchill. As a result of his waffling, the British were able to hold neither place. Most dramatic were the interventions in the debate of Leopold Amery and David Lloyd George. Amery, a Conservative, invoked against Chamberlain Oliver Cromwell's wrathful dismissal of the Rump Parliament: "You have sat too long for any good you do. Begone I say and let us have done. In the name of God, go!" Lloyd George, in one of his rare appearances in the House, had seen this all before. "The Prime Minister has called for sacrifice," he observed. "He should give an example for there is nothing which he can contribute more to victory in this war than that he should sacrifice his seals of office." After some hesitation, fearing the strength of Conservative party discipline, the Labour party forced a division on the afternoon of May 8.

The result destroyed Chamberlain. The Conservatives' usual majority, a huge 200 to 240 was reduced to 81 with 41 Conservatives voting against Chamberlain's government and about another 60 abstaining. This was a massive defection, a turnover of 140 votes, more than sufficient to bring down any administration in normal times.

Chamberlain did not want to resign. For forty-eight hours he busily canvassed the possibilities of a coalition. The Labour party, after two decades of abuse, now had its revenge upon him and refused to serve in any ministry headed by him. On May 10 he presided over a Cabinet in the morning and saw the King in the afternoon. In his enquiries he had encountered much sentiment for making Lord Halifax, the Foreign Secretary, Prime Minister. The King proposed Halifax, and Chamberlain himself might have preferred him in normal times. Halifax was a statesman of immense political experience and, as the Cabinet minutes show, within the privacy of the government counted by no means as an unqualified supporter of appeasement. But the times were not normal, even for war. At dawn on May 10 the German army had invaded Belgium and the Netherlands in massive force. Although Chamberlain believed for a moment that this event meant he should stay, the man who matched the hour was Winston Churchill who had refused to serve under Halifax. With a fortitude no one ever questioned he possessed, Chamberlain proposed that George VI call upon Churchill to form a government, and a few hours later, still on May 10, consented to be a part of it himself.

Churchill records in his war memoirs that as he prepared for bed in the early hours of May 11, after a long day of Cabinet making, he felt a deep sense of relief and satisfaction. All his life had been but a preparation for that moment. One is left with the impression he regarded his succession as inevitable. This certainly was not the case. Even the Conservatives who did not dislike him personally and who admitted his courage, distrusted his judgment, indeed his mental balance, and were put off by his arrogance and his unwillingness to see any point of view but his own. He was blamed for leaving the Conservative party, for returning to it, and for behaving like a spoiled child whether in or out of the party. Churchill at the beginning of his tenure was able to preside as Prime Minister only because Chamberlain took office in his government, remained leader of the Conservative party, and demanded obedience from the rank and file. Not many men so unceremoniously ejected from office could have brought themselves to this. H. H. Asquith, under remarkably similar circumstances in December 1916, was unable to do so and destroyed his party. Churchill had offered Lloyd George the Ministry of Agriculture in his government. Chamberlain blocked it.

Chamberlain served as Leader of the Party and Lord President of the Council in Churchill's War Cabinet until October 3, 1940 when he resigned on account of health. He died a little more than a month later on November 10. Like a number of men who have seen their careers and life-work suddenly smashed, he was killed by cancer.

THE THIRD PHASE:
THE BATTLE OF FRANCE

Churchill had been appointed Prime Minister late on May 10, 1940, and had in fact filled the most important offices of his Cabinet by evening. That morning the Germans had invaded the Low Countries. The Belgian government, which, like the Norwegian, had hitherto refused any cooperation with the Allies, naturally promptly called for their help. However, the French command had assumed for years that a German move to the west would come through Belgium and so was prepared to send the bulk of its field army north together with the British Expeditionary Forces. Within three days they were engaged. On May 14, the Dutch army, which, unlike the Belgian, had been taken totally by surprise, was ordered by its commander to cease resistance. The Dutch government and Queen Wilhelmina herself went to Britain and continued the war.

Suddenly it became clear that Germany's attack on Belgium had been only a feint. It was a matador's cape held in the German right hand to draw the bull, while the sword was in the left hand, wrote General Eric von Manstein who devised the plan. The Allied forces, enticed into Belgium, found themselves cut off by fast-moving German armored divisions, which crossed the Meuse River at the city of Sedan over 100 miles to the east on May 13. Within a week, driving west up the valley of the Somme River, the Germans reached the English Channel and had isolated Allied forces in Belgium.

The dangers from this encirclement were compounded on May 26 when King Leopold of the Belgians, without notifying the French and British, surrendered the Belgian army, nearly one-half the Allied force. The Allied situation now moved from desperate to hopeless; evacuation was imperative before the Allies were overrun.

So began the miracle of Dunkirk, the famous mobilization of a rescue fleet of small boats, from small civilian pleasure craft to ancient Thames ferries to destroyers, which between May 28 and June 4 was able to lift off 338,000 men, most of the B.E.F., and over 100,000 French. Dunkirk was unquestionably a triumph of typically British improvisation. But the Flanders campaign, to which it provided the conclusion, was nonetheless a disastrous defeat. In simplest terms the British army had left behind nearly all its equipment. The men were home, but all the carefully hoarded tanks, artillery, trucks, and gun carriers, two years of production, were in German hands. And when the Germans had defeated France, as they easily accomplished by June 18, Britain would have to fight alone.

Historically, the almost effortless elimination of the French army in the six weeks between May 10 and June 18 may have offered an unpleasant but hugely important lesson for the Allies: that Hitler possessed an excellent army. Though Allied intelligence surely underestimated it after Poland and Norway, after May and June of 1940 there could be no doubt. In Belgium and France Hitler's troops fought at a serious disadvantage. They possessed 2,500 tanks to the Allies 3,600 far heavier tanks while fielding about the same number of men—about 600,000—though the Germans were theoretically not as well trained. All of this was more than made up by their almost total command of the air, except over Dunkirk, and by the immense German technical superiority in planning, staff work, organization, and battlefield communication. Hitler had achieved exactly what the Schlieffen plan had postulated for the Kaiser's army in 1914: the destruction of the French armies in six weeks. To employ Herbert Kitchener's incorrect prediction of 1914, in 1940 they had "marched through the French army like partridges."

It should be emphasized that, barring some units of the French First Army which had defended the beachhead at Dunkirk with much gallantry, so permitting the British evacuation, the French army had not been defeated in any normal sense. It had simply collapsed. Many units were left sitting on trains. Many others had surrendered without engagement. To this day it is impossible to find in French military archives any statistics on French battle deaths between May 10 and June 18, 1940. They are always mixed with total casualties, which include prisoners (and, of course, are huge) or with total deaths for the entire war. Presumably, the summer 1940 figures of battle deaths are embarrassingly small.

For the British the very magnitude of the German advances of the summer of 1940 obliterated the detachment and cynicism of the previous nine months. In retrospect it is easy to say that the idea the war would be won easily—which Chamberlain believed—was not only incorrect militarily, but was also bad public relations. However, an important factor in Britain's changing attitude was the presence of Winston Churchill. He wiped out everything that had gone before, and the war was begun again. If he understood little of the nuances of constituency politics, Churchill comprehended battlefield realities perfectly. In his first speeches as Prime Minister to the House of Commons and to the nation over radio, when the Battle of

France had only begun, he predicted untold dangers and sacrifice. In perhaps his most moving wartime statement, he warned the House of Commons to prepare for the fall of France and for the invasion of Britain. Even with most of Europe within the odious grasp of the Gestapo, Britain would go on to the end, "if necessary alone." "We shall fight in France, we shall fight on the seas and oceans, we shall fight with growing confidence and growing strength in the air, we shall defend our island whatever the cost may be. We shall fight on the beaches, we shall fight on the landing grounds, we shall fight in the fields and in the streets, we shall fight in the hills; we shall never surrender. . . ."

Two weeks later, on June 18, he announced to the nation on the BBC that resistance in France would end. "What General Weygand has called the Battle of France is over. I expect that the Battle of Britain is about to begin. Upon this battle depends the survival of Christian civilisation." And he concluded with the stirring declaration: "Let us therefore brace ourselves to our duty and so bear ourselves that if the British Empire and its Commonwealth lasts for a thousand years men will still say, 'This was their finest hour.'" That afternoon, June 18, the anniversary of Waterloo, appeared in the *Evening Standard* David Low's most famous cartoon, a single British soldier in battle dress, standing on a rocky headland overlooking the sea, holding a rifle and shaking his fist in defiance at a stormy sky, which appears to be crowded with airplanes. The caption was simply: "Very well, alone."

Churchill, aided certainly by Hitler and probably by incompetent French generalship, had accomplished a miracle, a turnabout in British devotion, ardor, and in the perception of the war. Instead of viewing the war as a resented inconvenience as it had six months earlier, the public now perceived it as a crusade. Whereas many people on the continent were settling down with an alacrity regretted later to the tranquility of peace, the British at last were prepared literally to do or die. Churchill's famous June 18 speech, the peroration quoted above, had begun with half an hour of hard, unpleasant facts about the nation's desperate position. The staff at 10 Downing Street thought it much too long and badly delivered. He sounded tired, which he was, although the world for more than a half century has found his words inspirational. But Churchill had taken the British people into his confidence in a way that governments seldom do. We must win he warned; "if we fail, then the whole world, including the United States . . . will sink into the abyss of a new dark age made more sinister, and perhaps more protracted, by the lights of a perverted science." These were frightening and challenging words, yet as the next five years would demonstrate, they were perfectly true. Britain must win or die.

In the end, Britain's place as the only survivor of the Allies seems to have brought to the nation, and clearly to Churchill, a kind of exhilaration. Decisions became simpler, as they always do in war, but in coalitions allies must be consulted. Now there were none. For Churchill the removal of the dead weight of the French, who had seemed unwilling to do anything to provoke the Germans, was obviously a relief. He provided an example of the new sharpened determination almost immediately. On July 3, 1940, the British Mediterranean fleet attacked and destroyed a number of major units of the French fleet in the harbor of Oran in Algeria to prevent their appropriation by the Germans. Well over 1,200 French sailors were killed in a nine-minute bombardment. Such an attack, upon a force that six weeks before had been fighting by the side of the Royal Navy, was emphatically not the work of a defeated nation. Further, it revealed a bloody-mindedness that so far had been conspicuously absent from Britain's war effort. When Churchill entered the House of Commons to report on the African operation the Conservative Members enthusiastically cheered him for the first time. On his first appearance as Prime Minister on May 13, the Conservatives had cheered not Churchill, but Chamberlain.

THE FOURTH PHASE:
THE BATTLE OF BRITAIN

The flame at the core of the new British resolve lay in the threat of a German invasion. The German preparation for such an assault need not be discussed here, except to say that the British military's perception of the German power was greater than its reality. Indeed both sides far overestimated the other's military capabilities. Hitler had never expected an invasion to be necessary. There existed no plans for one. The assumption during the first war, upon which indeed the Germans based their grand strategy in the West, had been that if France could be forced from the war Britain would negotiate a compromise peace.

Accordingly, Hitler dawdled on formal invasion planning while issuing between mid-June and mid-July a number of gradually more explicit invitations to Britain to come to some sort of accommodation with Germany. "His heart was not in it," observed German General Eric von Manstein. Not until July 16 was there a clear order to prepare for an invasion. At this time the German army discovered that the German navy could not promise to deliver and supply anything approaching the number of men the High Command felt necessary for the quick conquest of Britain. In a nutshell, invasion planning never proceeded beyond this impasse, although the Germans began to collect barges and to practice amphibious landing techniques.

There was however one requirement for a successful invasion upon which army and navy could agree: Germany must have command of the air over the English Channel and over the British Isles. Accordingly, an air attack could begin immediately while the services haggled over ways and means. The Battle of Britain began as the first stage of a projected German invasion.

One cannot give a date for the beginning of the battle. Through May and June 1940 the *Luftwaffe* had been attacking shipping in the English Channel and port facilities on the east and south coasts with increasing vigor. In mid-June, as the fighting in France ended, it moved to attacks on inland towns although these were uncoordinated and without pattern. At the same time the Germans began to suffer serious losses. On August 1 Hitler ordered a concentrated attack upon the Royal Air Force itself, upon the sector stations (airfields) and radar installations instead of harbors and food storage facilities. The intent was to bring the entire British Fighter Command into battle so that German superiority in numbers could wear it down.

These attacks began however, only on August 13, the date German histories customarily assign to the beginning of the Battle of Britain. This was a massive strike against R.A.F. airfields in southeast England by nearly 1,500 German aircraft, of which about 1,000 were fighters. Losses were heavy on both sides. The massive bombing of airfields continued for about a month, through the first two weeks of September. By this time the R.A.F., defending itself and Britain, approached exhaustion. Its losses, though heavy, were rarely as much as two-thirds the German casualties. To be sure, the R.A.F. was fighting among its own people; pilots of disabled airplanes could parachute to earth to be helped by a friendly population. Conversely, the German airmen became prisoners and were sometimes treated as savages. To Britain's anger, the French, in haste to make peace after June 18, had returned to Germany 400 *Luftwaffe* pilots, mostly shot down by the R.A.F. Meanwhile, the R.A.F. was running short of fighter pilots.

The rule of thumb in Britain and the United States during the second war held that a pilot's training consumed a year and required 600 or 700 hours in the air. Such a process could not be hurried, although in the United States pilot training—primary, basic, and advanced—for a time in 1943 was reduced to nine months. In September 1940 aircraft were being manufactured far more rapidly than pilots could be trained to fly them, and many were stored on the palace grounds at Windsor. By the end of the summer nearly 500 new fighter aircraft were being delivered per month, matching almost exactly the rate of losses.

But the replacement figures for pilots were dismal. During the two weeks from August 24 to September 6 when the attack on the R.A.F. installations was at its height, 295 fighters had been destroyed, but were replaced by 269 new or fully repaired airplanes. On the other hand during the same fortnight 103 pilots had been killed and another 123 seriously wounded to be replaced by about 120 newly trained men, a reduction of more than 109 in total Fighter Command strength of about 1,000. Put another way a squadron's establishment was twenty-six pilots. The average active roster during August 1940 was sixteen.

There were two further complications in the air war. The efficiency of experienced pilots decreased under the stress of continued flying. Four or five scrambles a day caused tension that began to affect eyesight and sense of balance. Second, more serious, was the high rate of losses in air combat among replacements. New men too frequently were killed before they acquired the necessary fighting skills for survival. At the end of August

1940 Air Chief Marshall Sir Hugh Dowding of Fighter Command could reflect that German superiority in nothing but manpower was bleeding his organization to death. No matter what were the statistics of British aircraft production, or of the ratio of losses among the R.A.F. as opposed to those of the *Luftwaffe*, the Germans were winning. If one mistake were made, such as the surprise of a large number of British planes refuelling (caught on the ground), the air battle would all be over. Like Admiral John Jellicoe in 1916, Dowding knew he could lose the war in an afternoon.

On September 7 the Germans now changed their target to metropolitan London, inadvertently saving the R.A.F., although that was not immediately clear. The reasons for the German adoption of new tactics are not as simple as they once had seemed. The British had bombed Berlin on August 25, causing little damage but much anger, and the German attack upon London thirteen days later was assumed to be a result of this. There is some truth to that. German propaganda did proclaim the London attacks to be retaliatory, but the new tactics were prompted also by the apparent failure of the *Luftwaffe* seriously to diminish the fighting power of the R.A.F.. The Germans were in fact confused by their own inflated statistics, which if taken seriously showed that the R.A.F. had been destroyed twice over and that the *Luftwaffe* had won. Yet the red and black British Spitfires diving out of the sun seemed always to be there. The Germans did not know how close they actually were to victory. Whatever the reason, on September 7, London, hitherto exempt, began to suffer massive daylight raids by multiple flights of 200 or more bombers, heavily escorted by Messerschmitt fighters.

The daylight attacks upon London, essentially between September 7 and October 5 stretched German air power beyond its limit. Statistical evidence demonstrates this clearly enough. According to Churchill's record, in the week ending September 7 the R.A.F. lost 144 airplanes, the highest wastage of the Battle of Britain, while the Luftwaffe lost, by German record, 187. In the following week, the first week of the attacks on London, even though the Germans lost fewer aircraft, 102, the R.A.F. losses fell to 67, less than one-half the previous week's. In the following week, which included the climactic Sunday of

September 15 (now Battle of Britain Day) the *Luftwaffe* casualties rose to 120 and the Royal Air Force's fell to 52.

While these first weeks of September resulted in much concentrated destruction, particularly in London's East End and dockland, they marked, nevertheless, the beginning of the end of the Battle of Britain. The Germans found that London was beyond the practical range of their fighter escorts. At their most economical speed the early Messerschmitts had a range of 410 miles. The closest German airfields were almost 100 miles from London and most were further. Moreover, once within R.A.F. airspace incoming German aircraft could not fly at low speeds, and aerial combat used gasoline at a frightening rate. The inevitable result of a single burst of fire into a fuel tank from the eight-machine guns carried by a British Spitfire meant ditching in the English Channel. Therefore, the German pilots fought cautiously.

It worked out that German fighter pilots flying to London could expect at best a time over target of about ten minutes. This frequently meant being forced to leave the bombers they were supposed to protect while in the midst of combat. By themselves the lightly armed bombers were almost defenseless, which accounts for the huge losses quoted above. Adolph Galland, who would become the perfect knight of the *Luftwaffe*, tells in his memoirs of the plunging pilot morale that followed the concentration on London. The contrast with the mood in Germany was devastating.

Throughout the continent, September 1940 had provided for some a sense of relief, almost of gaiety. The war no one wanted had come to an end. Diarists supplement these observations. In Germany theaters reopened, rations increased, and plans were announced for the demobilization of reserve divisions. For the Germans, Paris in the lambent, cloudless summer of 1940 was a magnet for tourists. Families visited sons and fathers and, above all, shopped. Of course goods soon disappeared from the shelves, but in 1940 the German mark would buy anything. Officers' clubs were established. There were hunts and grand receptions. The French Resistance, much celebrated after the war, was not yet born. Britain, said General Maxime Weygand, who had insisted upon the surrender of France, "would have its neck wrung like a chicken." Accommodation of Germany within the New Europe (designated over the radio as "Greater Germany") was the rule and was quietly welcomed especially since it meant an end to war. Galland's bitterness is clear. Out on the Channel coasts, as weather turned worse in September and Reichsmarschal Hermann Göering personally took charge of the London attack, German morale slumped. New faces appeared at the airmen's mess table and then quickly disappeared. The veterans could calculate on their fingers the declining odds against their own survival. Yet back at home the German people assumed the war was over.

BRITAIN IN GLOBAL WAR

October 1940 to December 1941

On September 17, two days after the disastrous Sunday raid on London in which German losses proved to be well over twice those suffered by the R.A.F., Hitler ordered the postponement of invasion preparations, and on October 12 the invasion was cancelled "for the winter." More important, on October 20, the daylight bombing of London ended, to be replaced by intensive night attacks by unescorted bombers. The undirected bombardment of London, as well as of other British cities, became known as the "Blitz."

The Blitz was hardly a military operation. At best it was an act of boastfulness by Reichsmarschal Göering, at worst an admission of failure. The *Luftwaffe* had failed to gain mastery of the air over Britain without which an invasion was impossible. In the nine months that it continued, about 30,000 civilians were killed, more than half in London. Life became hideously uncomfortable and one-third of London's stock of houses was destroyed or damaged. But Britain's capacity to make war was hardly affected. With the beginnings of large-scale American aid under the Lend Lease program in the spring of 1941 and with the energetic mobilization of industrial resources that began under Churchill's administration, when the Blitz ended in May of 1941, Britain was immensely stronger than it had been at the time of the German attack in the West the year before. To be sure, Hitler retained the initiative as he demonstrated on June 22, 1941, when his armies attacked the Soviet Union. Yet even while the Blitz was at its height, British and Imperial forces had driven the Italians, who entered the war on June 10, 1940 (on the side of the Germans), from Ethiopia, Somalia, and Eritrea, so-called Italian East Africa, and thoroughly defeated and routed the huge Italian army in Libya. Although alone, Britain had achieved the first Allied land victories of the war.

The luster of these successes was dimmed in April and May 1941 by Britain's failure to prevent the German conquest of Greece and the island of Crete. An expeditionary force sent to the Aegean was overwhelmed by German paratroops, albeit with terrible losses. But only about one-half the British force returned to Africa.

Nonetheless, heroic and successful as was the year 1941, the beginning of the war against the U.S.S.R., followed six months later by Japan's attack upon the United States, meant that Britain's central place in the resistance to Nazism would diminish. One must imagine that Churchill sensed this. Much as he welcomed the addition of powerful partners in the war and warm as were his personal relations with President Franklin Roosevelt, his impatience with his obviously deteriorating authority is clear in his letters and memoranda. His frustration, his secretaries report, occasionally drove him to tears of selfpity that could be kept up for several minutes. But then a new idea would come, the eyes would gleam, he would reach for a cigar and a map. He was back in the war. President Roosevelt fully concurred with the American command in its refusal of logistical support for British adventures in the eastern Mediterranean. An American, Dwight Eisenhower, not Sir Allen Brooke, Chief of the Imperial General Staff, became commander of the Allied Expeditionary Force. Later, to Churchill's fury, Eisenhower refused to allow the Prime Minister to go on board a command ship of the invasion fleet on June 6, 1944 to watch the landing in Normandy. Surely Churchill came to look back fondly on the year that Britain stood alone and within his charge, perilous as that year had been.

After 1941, even though Churchill could say that with the adherence of the United States Britain could not lose the war,

Britain's fate, not to mention that of western civilization, was tied intimately to the endurance of the Soviet Union. Had Stalin's empire collapsed, as it was close to doing in the week that the Japanese attacked, making Hitler the master of Soviet resources, the European conflict might have become something akin to a war of the worlds. In such a battle, Britain's part would have been very small.

8 / THE WAR EXPERIENCE

WARTIME POLITICS

After the formation of what Winston Churchill referred to as the Grand Alliance, Britain's military history became simply a part of the story of the fortunes of a coalition with which it would rise or fall. Britain's armies and fleets marched and sailed in response to decisions no longer made solely in London. Aggravating as all of this may have been to Churchill, whose personal attention was focused almost entirely upon the war, it inevitably constituted an unpleasant fact of his life. Britain's fate lay no longer in its own hands. For the student of British history, therefore, a more profitable study may reside in the evolution of affairs within the British Isles, upon the revolution in politics that occurred during the war. These changes were linked in folk memories both to the broken pledges of a "better Britain" made during the last phase of the Great War and as well to the unforgotten hardship of the decade of the 1930s, when a generation of young men and women had grown up without the experience or even the promise of economic security.

The linked traditions of hard times and of a perceived Conservative indifference to the popular welfare became a fixture of British workers' wartime culture. Evidence of the phenomena began to be noted in opinion polls and in investigations of popular attitudes sponsored by the Ministry of Information as early as the spring of 1941, as the Blitz began to recede. An initial response that particularly worried the government appeared in marked voter indifference to politics. Even though with rationing, air raid precautions, and labor control, state regulation touched the citizen in a score of ways entirely unknown before, his concern for ordinary parliamentary and party affairs seemed to have vanished. Most voters did not know the name of their MP. Nor with the exception of Churchill and Ernest Bevin could they name any member of the Cabinet. When asked his opinion of politicians as a group, a respondent usually expressed scorn accompanied by remarks about selfishness and corruption. Linked with these attitudes appeared a surge in the popularity of the Soviet Union that grew more pronounced in the spring of 1942 as it became clear that the Russians would not quickly be defeated by the Germans. This admiration soon translated into a widespread demand for a second front in France, an operation for which neither Britain nor the United States was in any way prepared. Nonetheless, it caused endless trouble for the War Cabinet.

A corollary to the admiration for Soviet courage manifested itself by the summer of 1942 in a dislike of Americans. This again was a difficult problem for the Churchill administration. (A private, not a government, poll found in July 1942 that 62 percent of the respondents thought the Soviet Union more popular than the United States; 24 percent thought the opposite.) People were clearly happy that the United States had entered the war, were willing to concede many good qualities to it as a nation, while Churchill worked mightily to explain the critical importance of the tremendous gift of Lend Lease, which had saved Britain from bankruptcy if not starvation. But individual American soldiers, who began to appear in large numbers in the summer of 1942, were not always welcomed nor admired. There seem to have been no systematic polls, but the sentiment is clear from diaries and letters across all classes, from Harold Nicolson, MP, a thin and weedy sort himself, who denigrated the physique of American G.I.'s, to the diaries of soldiers who found discourtesy in pubs and refusal of service in restaurants. The catch-phrase popular at the time summed it up: "They're over-paid, they're over-sexed, and they're over here." All of this grew worse as the American presence in Britain increased into the millions in the last years of the war. The resentment of Americans by Britons, who found themselves being patronized by members of a society to which they had always believed themselves superior, was only a part of something that may be seen as a tidal change in public attitudes. It was as if the ordinary man's evolving perception of the world around him had come to a complete stop and had then begun to move again in a new, and unexpected, direction.

To gain perspective one should examine the differences between the reaction of society to the first and to the second war. This essay has as a thesis that in Britain the impact of the first war was greater. The sufferer in the first war, besides the families of 750,000 men killed and a million more wounded, was Great Britain as a whole, the nation and its place in the world. It lost the economic dominion that it had enjoyed for more than a century. This decline had begun before the first war, but the war had converted a slow trickle into a deluge, and the British worker suffered on account of it through the 1920s and 1930s. Worse, after the first war the nation asked not for reform but for a return to the prewar world, in effect nostalgia. As has been seen, Stanley Baldwin became the beneficiary of this nostalgia.

The consequences of the backward-looking complacency that followed the first war were huge, but somehow unrecognized. Britons still considered their nation a first-class power and the government behaved accordingly. The consensus that Edwardian Britain could be somehow resurrected precluded any planning or adjustment to altered conditions. Rather no change was required. It was hoped that the City would take again its pre-eminent place, trade would be rebuilt, society and class restored. Great Britain remained the axle of the universe. There was a sense of charade about all of this, as if Britain were an old couple inhabiting a huge semiderelict mansion from which much of the furniture had been sold and most servants were gone, while the owners clung still to the traditional ceremonies, the accustomed dress, and the old habits.

The impact of the second war on society was entirely different. For Britain the second war lasted for nearly six years, two years longer than the first, and long enough for it to become a normal part of daily existence. Battlefield casualties were a quarter of those in the first war and national mobilization was far more rigorous. Many observers, including a future Prime Minister, found almost a contentment among the working population. By 1943 the war itself was routine, something one read of in the newspapers. Food was boring, clothing difficult to buy, housing cramped, but for millions of workers these conditions were no worse than the 1930s. Instead there was economic security and a shared sense of deprivation, a state of being never experienced before. Everyone contributed, everyone was at risk. The second war was, as it frequently has been termed, a people's, not only a soldiers', war. Its dramatic moment, the Battle of

Britain, although an unbelievable accomplishment by 1,000 fighter pilots, remained a people's victory, and church bells, appropriately, rang when it ended. More to the point, the second war had brought to an end not a period of relatively stable prosperity but to eighteen years of poverty and squalor. There was no nostalgia after the second war. The thirties were not worth going back to. Rather, the nation, with healthy realism, demanded new departures, new ideas.

These conditions certainly account for the tumultuous, popular welcome given to the November 1942 report by Sir William Beveridge on Britain's social welfare institutions, which the government found embarrassing. Their discomfiture at the document proceeded from the fact that the report was less a survey of existing services, which they had asked for, than a plan for overhauling social services into a unified system for the protection of the entire population. This was not at all what the government had expected.

The Beveridge report originated in a not untypical civil service intrigue that compounded the government's detestation of its contents. Although Beveridge was a distinguished scholar and writer on social problems, his vanity and arrogance had long since earned him a reputation as an impossible colleague both in government and academe. He could get along with no one. In the spring of 1941 his antagonist was his minister at Labour and National Service, the second most powerful man in the Churchill coalition government, Ernest Bevin. Bevin needed little time after he came to the ministry in October, 1940, to realize that Beveridge would have to go, and it appears that the investigation of the effect of the war on social services was invented to give Beveridge something to do.

Thus the Beveridge report was born an orphan, loved by no one except Sir William himself and the working population of Great Britain. It provides the one big political story of the war and was surely an important factor in Churchill's defeat in 1945. On one hand, the plan called for a dangerous, practically unthinkable, commitment in the midst of a desperate war, that in 1942 was by no means won. Beveridge's cost estimates were certainly too low, and no one could predict the condition of the country at the war's end. On the other hand, it was obviously a superb piece of wartime propaganda, which Beveridge understood fully and used with great skill. It gave meaning to the nation's war effort. It promised that peace would bring not only military victory, but economic security. It seemed to show, despite the popular consensus to the contrary, that those in authority did care about the common man.

Here lay an absurd dilemma. The government could not accept the report. Indeed, Churchill forbade such action. But neither could it be disavowed. The result was a clumsy prevarication. The Beveridge report was given the widest possible publicity. Nearly 700,000 copies were printed by the Stationery Office and it was fully discussed in newspapers. But ministers were forbidden to mention it. In the House of Commons, which had been allowed only to "take note" of the report as a "guide" to future legislation, questions were answered uniformly with the statement that it was under study. Beveridge, who found himself a public hero and according to polls the best known man in the Kingdom after Winston Churchill, discovered also that he was literally barred from government offices. Civil servants were afraid to speak to him or even to be seen with him.

The Beveridge report must be looked at in the context of the time. For practical purposes the war had adjourned politics. By-elections were not contested by the major parties. The government contained all parties. Within the comprehensiveness of national mobilization almost anything could be justified as a military necessity, and unanimity was required. But Beveridge split the coalition neatly and visibly, giving Labour a solid issue to seize upon in 1945. At the same time, it would be wrong to say that the Labour party after 1945 built the welfare state upon the Beveridge plan. Ernest Bevin, who could not endure Beveridge's vanity and rudeness and who was by far the senior lieutenant in Clement Attlee's government, insisted upon some important changes as did other ministers. The Beveridge report was hardly the blueprint for the National Insurance Act of 1946, an assumption often made by historians. It was a major political event during the war and a factor in the 1945 election, but much less important as a pattern for future legislation.

ECONOMICS

The British, one may comment, proclaim political democracy, but are more than dubious about social equality. A good deal used to be made of the comradeship of the trenches as a leveling force in the first war that wiped out traditional class snobbery. How much of this is true is hard to say—the officer's batman (a kind of valet) remained apparent—but there can be no doubt that social class pretensions returned quickly enough in the 1920s. In this respect the impact of the second war was more profound and longer lasting.

The war of 1939–45 began at a time when Britain was in the grip of a long and agonizing economic depression. Many men already in their thirties had never in their lives known the security of permanent employment. The war provided unlimited employment, although rather more slowly than might have been expected. Perhaps the greatest leveling force was civilian mobilization. The heavy hand of national service, the near-total price control and rationing of most items of civilian consumption, an income and surtax that took over two-thirds of a bachelor's income at £10,000, and above all the vast, but almost unplanned, expansion of social services, certainly blurred the differences in living standards in Britain for all but the wealthiest. After admitting quickly that class distinction is not entirely a function of money, one must emphasize that money helps a lot and that inherited money helps most of all. Still the second war brought equality, a sense of social equity, to Britain that the first had never done. The rich were visibly pushed down, and many workers were in fact better off. Money simply meant less; coupons were what counted. With gasoline rationing the well-to-do had to take their place on buses and the underground; men's woolen clothing was controlled to the point of disappearance. Conversely, the poorer classes, particularly the urban poor and above all their children, found available a multitude of unusual goods and services furnished in the name of national health and fitness by a newly enlightened government which was convinced that these qualities were essential to winning the war. Much of the distribution was done through schools. Children were provided with milk and orange juice practically unobtainable otherwise, and with lunches either free or at nominal charge. Similarly, their parents received specially subsidized meals in factory canteens, which received special rations as well. A widespread notion during the war held that the only decent meals in Britain were to be found in the factories.

A more dramatic, almost accidental, change in the social services brought on by the war lay in the provision of medical care. In the period covered by this essay, Britain's workers had access to a variety of public and charitable medical institutions, none of which had much relation to each other. Few offered a comprehensive service. People earning less than £240 per year, the starting point of the income tax, were covered by National Health Insurance, which provided the worker with general practitioner care and a small sickness benefit, but which, with some exceptions, offered no specialist or hospital treatment nor anything for dependents. For serious illness the worker or his family could resort to the voluntary hospitals (i.e. nonprofit, similar to most "general" hospitals in the United States). Some of these, the teaching hospitals in the major cities, were excellent, famous, and crowded. However, after waiting several hours in the outpatient clinic a worker's child could be seen by a Harley Street specialist, free of charge. If the child needed inpatient care there would be eventually a bed in a ward at a fee determined by the hospital almoner.

Finally there were the old Poor Law hospitals, which had come into being in the early nineteenth century as infirmaries for the workhouse but which by the turn of the twentieth century had become in some cases, mostly in London, large, decently modern hospitals. Of course many of them remained a resort for chronically ill elderly who had no place else to go. The Old Age Pension Act of 1908 had been intended to address exactly this problem.

In the interwar years Chamberlain's Local Government Act of 1929, among other things, had permitted the municipal governments to take over and operate the Poor Law infirmaries as municipal hospitals, but only in London had this been done systematically. When the war came the former Poor Law institutions were by far the most accessible resort for secondary medical treatment for five-sixths of the British population. While a decent number of them possessed by 1939 large staffs of competent physicians using modern equipment, there was still about them the atmosphere, one could almost say the odor, of the despised Poor Law. Their patients were still counted in the statistics of pauperism. The county and borough council committees that operated them were patronizingly called Guardians Committees, even though the relief they provided was officially Public Assistance.

The war changed all of this. With the creation in 1939 of the Emergency Medical Services (E.M.S.), the Chamberlain government brought into being an institution that became the direct ancestor of the huge National Health Service. Like so much else at the beginning of the war, the E.M.S. was a part of the expectation of, indeed the fixation upon, round-the-clock aerial bombardment. Hospitals were ordered to discharge, peremptorily, their chronic but nonterminal patients. Further, they were required to set aside a proportion of their beds for air-raid victims, usually about 10 percent, for which the government would pay a fee whether the beds were occupied or not. Grouped into regions around large cities based upon a teaching hospital, they were to establish casualty treatment stations staffed by specialists who would be reimbursed by the government and to put together ambulance services for the quick evacuation of wounded to the countryside. Meanwhile, the government began a large program to resupply hospitals with the most modern diagnostic equipment, chest x-ray machines and the like, for the treatment of traumatic and orthopedic wounds.

The Blitz lasted eight months, with a revival in the summer and autumn of 1944 caused by the buzz bomb and rocket attacks. But the grimly anticipated horde of civilian wounded never appeared. Altogether, the Battle of Britain and the Blitz resulted in 43,000 civilian dead and 53,000 injured, about one-half of those in London. The V-1s, the "buzz bombs," killed 5,500 in three months from June 12 to September 5, 1944, and left 16,000 injured, because they exploded on contact. The V-2, the rocket attacks, began on September 12, 1944, and lasted until the end of November. As the V-2s tended to penetrate before exploding, they caused 2,700 casualties, nearly all deaths.

Without clients the Emergency Medical Service became a problem instead of a solution. It constituted a large, hugely expensive facility, put together in the frantic days of prewar terror, which now had almost lost its function. The government response was to open the E.M.S. to classes other than those for whom it had been intended. The list grew throughout the war. Wounds from enemy action were no longer necessary for admission. Families, the tens of thousands "bombed out" who were living in shelters, and those who contracted contagious illnesses, were admitted. Soon, war workers and then families of war workers in factories away from home, as well as families of serving soldiers not covered by military medical care, became acceptable. In fact, anyone who was affected by the war could, in the end, use the E.M.S. As there were very few who were not affected in one way or another by the war, the numbers turned away were small. By the spring of 1945 Britain had something approximating universal health coverage. Most important, it included dependent, hospital, and specialist care.

Thus the second war achieved, almost accidentally and clearly without any enthusiasm from the Churchill Cabinet, the revolution in British social services that had failed to materialize after the first war. The E.M.S. provided the political leverage that forced both political parties to include in their manifestos a pledge for a unified, comprehensive, and all-inclusive, medical care. It was simply unthinkable that after three years of free, or rather taxpayer-supported, medical care, such a system should disappear. Welfare services, far more than any other form of government activity, operate with a rachet effect: a benefit once provided may not be withdrawn unless replaced by something better. Hence they can only grow larger. Examples of this phenomenon are innumerable, both in Britain and the United States. In 1945 there was little to distinguish the plans of the Conservative and Labour parties except for the detail, albeit a major one, of the nationalization of the voluntary hospitals. It is worth recalling that a comprehensive medical service was not part of the Beveridge plan, as is often assumed, except for a single line in which Sir William took for granted that one would be established.

As the war drew to a close the British people lived in a state of economic equality certainly unknown within living memory. The fears that war and submarine blockade would degrade the nation's health—perhaps an influenza epidemic as a consequence of malnutrition—proved to be unfounded. All the sensitive indicators of vitality: longevity, paranatal and infant mortality, improved markedly. Britain emerged from the war perhaps a hungrier, but healthier nation than before. Before the war a large number had fed too well, doctored too well, indeed lived too well. But many more received less than enough. Between 1940 and 1945 the high and low ends of this continuum had been visibly diminished. As the general election campaign began in the spring of 1945, the Labour party showed that it understood what had happened. Its slogans "Fair Shares For All" and "Don't Let Them Take It Away" aimed precisely at the beneficiaries of the wartime social revolution. One could add that the popular acceptance of the new egalitarianism made possible, with surprisingly little dissent, the continuation of wartime restriction and rationing into the 1950s under the title of "Austerity."

THE ELECTION OF 1945; THE REPUDIATION OF OLDE ENGLAND

The General Election of July 5, 1945, represented a recognition, perhaps a celebration, of the new equality. At the time the defeat of Winston Churchill was a surprise and a shock, not least to Churchill himself. Viewed in perspective it seems to have been inevitable.

The public disenchantment with politics and politicians that appeared very early in the war already has been noted. But no one among the Conservatives seems to have worried greatly. The important fact was that Churchill's personal approval rating, carefully measured every month from the beginning of his incumbency, stood and remained consistently above 80 percent and occasionally touched 90 percent. In May, 1945 in the last poll of the series as the election campaign began, 83 percent of the sample approved of the way Churchill handled his job. The general assumption, shared by Conservative and Labour leaders and certainly by Clement Attlee, Labour's Prime Minister-designate, who admitted as much, held that any party or combination headed by Churchill could not lose.

Yet in the same May 1945, as Churchill announced a coming election, voters asked how they would vote were an election held at that time responded 45 percent to 33 percent for Labour over the Conservatives with only 5 percent undecided. These figures were little changed from responses given two years earlier in the summer of 1943 as the African campaign ended and the invasion of Sicily began, in effect at the climax of the first series of important Allied victories. One senses that the 1943 polling figures were almost a response to these events. The nation had begun to look beyond the war. The government's reaction six months earlier to the Beveridge plan was at least ambiguous and still in the news. What would be the individual family's situation when the war ended? The existing political system was either feeble or corrupt. As Britain moved toward a victory both Labour majorities in the polls and Churchill's approval rating grew larger. The war had lasted for six years. By the time it ended, peace was not a normal state of affairs. Rather it was a departure, to be distrusted if not feared. Aneurin Bevan, a rising Labour radical who would become Minister of Health and create the National Health Service, caught the mood exactly in an important pamphlet entitled "Why Not Trust the Tories?" Bevan invited the questioner to remember the 1920s and 1930s.

Churchill, certainly one of the most inept political operators of the twentieth century but well provided with political information, may have sensed the prevailing turmoil. In any case, he attempted to avoid an election when Germany surrendered on May 8, 1945. He proposed to Clement Attlee on May 18 that the coalition government remain in office until the end of the war in the Far East, expected then to continue for another eighteen months. At the same time he warned that if Labour refused he would dissolve immediately. The Labour party, then in conference, declined to remain in office. They would allow the existing government to continue until October to permit arrangements to be made for a military vote and, no doubt more to the point, to allow the compilation of a new, badly needed, electoral register. There had been, of course, no general election since 1935. With the evacuation of the inner cities during the war, hundreds of thousands of Labour voters would not be able to cast ballots. No doubt Churchill, or at least his political advisor, Max Aitken,

Lord Beaverbrook, apprehended this fact as well. In any case, on May 23 Churchill resigned and announced a dissolution for June 15 with polling on July 5. He took office immediately at the head of a caretaker, single party, government.

Ministerial behavior, particularly Churchill's, during the short campaign that followed seriously offended the British electorate. Even though Labour surely would have won in any case, the Prime Minister's outrageous denunciations of men who had been loyal Cabinet colleagues a few days earlier, cost the government a substantial number of votes. Another complaint, apparent in polls taken after the election, lay in the perception that the Conservatives seemed to be attempting to run Churchill in every constituency. Probably the base of Labour's huge victory with an almost unprecedented turnover of seats can be found in this prejudice. Conservative party electoral tactics presented Churchill not only as the party leader but the party platform. "Help him finish the job" under the Prime Minster's portrait constituted their most visible piece of propaganda in every electoral district. Thus Churchill, a living relic of the old politics, was pitted against Labour's invocation of the sufferings of the 1920s and 1930s and its promise of a better world. He was a hero to be sure, but out-of-date. For most Britons with the surrender of Germany, the war was over, Japan notwithstanding. Yet the Conservatives foolishly allowed the Prime Minister's majestic presence to obscure their own very real plans for social security, giving away the symbol of the Beveridge proposals. Meanwhile Labour, with a leader whom hardly anyone had heard of in Clement Attlee, concentrated on the remembrance of past horrors and Beveridge's promise of future security.

The results announced on July 26, three weeks after the election to allow counting of the military vote, astounded everyone in both parties, even though the historian can say with customary assurance that the issue was never in doubt. Labour leaders simply had not believed the party preference data emerging during the war. Their constituency organizations were decayed, they argued. The old electoral register favored the Conservatives. Churchill's popularity was unprecedented. Nonetheless a Conservative majority in the House of Commons sank from 232 before the election to a Labour majority of 180, an unbelievable turnover of 412 seats in a House of Commons of 640.

Churchill was crushed, as his biographer, Martin Gilbert, describes. He had been in Berlin in a conference at Potsdam planning the fate of Europe with Joseph Stalin and the new American President Harry Truman. As the King's first minister—his own phrase—he had returned during the counting to observe and enjoy the expression of the confidence of the nation. Instead he discovered on the evening of July 26 that the British people had, as he put it, "dismissed [him] from all conduct of their affairs." Politics is not a gentle business.

The second war ended at a time when British potency in world affairs clearly had begun to decline. In the bipolar world of superpowers, as Foreign Secretary Anthony Eden's correspondence with Churchill demonstrates, both men believed their nation's best and proper place was as a mediator between east and west. Britain could employ its superior diplomatic craft to lend some sophistication to President Roosevelt's clumsy attempts to charm Joseph Stalin away from territorial hegemony won by Russian arms.

But even if Britain could still exert influence upon the United States, its power to project its will throughout the world had dissipated. In reality this omnipotence had disappeared in the Great War, but a quarter century lay between this reality and popular acknowledgment, although senior politicians understood it well enough. The sense of the nation's vulnerability remained constantly apparent in interwar Cabinet discussions and memoranda on foreign policy: over the coercion of Turkey at Chanak in 1922, which finally brought down Lloyd George; in the Anglo-German Naval Treaty; in the Royal Navy's shortage of ammunition in the Mediterranean during the Italian-Ethiopian War; and perhaps most clearly in the slow and inadequate rearming of Singapore, supposed to demonstrate concern for the protection of Australia and New Zealand. The Empire was no longer a glory but a burden.

At bottom, the problem reduced itself simply to loss of wealth or, more pointedly, to the decay of the productive facilities that produced wealth, combined with the changed public perceptions of the government's obligations toward the relief of hardship at home. All of this has been discussed at length. The cumulative effect, however, was that the navy, the overseas stations most of all, and the army, were tragically unprepared for the tasks assigned them by British diplomacy of the 1930s. The almost blind stubbornness of Winston Churchill, the skill and courage of the Royal Air Force, and the unbelievable errors of grand strategy committed by Germany and Japan, saved Britain from destruction. But even with the infamy of Hitler, Britain's weakness made the declaration of war in 1939 an act of reckless folly, as many men, from David Lloyd George to Captain B. H. Liddell Hart, understood.

Why had Britain not recovered from the Great War as Germany had done? The fault was partly its own, outlined in this essay: the unwillingness of the government to make use of inflation as all other European nations had done to pay the war debt or to employ inflation plus tariffs to stimulate production. Banking was accommodated at the expense of manufacturing. At least as important was the dissipation in the war of the worldwide pattern of markets from which Britain's accumulation of wealth had derived and upon which it, far more than any other major power, depended. With the markets had gone also the overseas investments that trading had produced. Since 1870 with a huge surplus in income earned abroad, British businessmen sensibly had not repatriated all profits earned overseas but had reinvested them in the countries from which the profits came. The destruction of overseas wealth in the first war was not perhaps so complete as the liquidation that occurred in the first two years of the second war as a consequence of the requirement of cash for British military purchases in the United States, but the liquidation in 1939–41 proceeded from a far smaller base in real terms. With the first war Britain moved from the esteemed 1914 position of the world's creditor to the humble place of its debtor by 1918 and remained there. That the Bank of England, representing in fact the British government, should in 1931 have to apply for gold, cap in hand, to the Federal Reserve Bank of New York demonstrated the lamentable consequences. In happier times the world, including the United States, came to London.

This essay, then, ends as it began, as a discussion of the impact upon Britain of two desperate world wars and of what happened between them. In thirty-one years, less than a generation, Britain devolved into a third-class power. In 1945, it was not a superpower, nor in fact even a match for Germany, nor probably France, let alone Japan, once these nations regained their feet. The nation may not have understood this fully until 1956 in the ill-starred Suez invasion when a decently successful military operation was brought down by, as always, economic pressure. Instead of being the master of the pound, once the world's currency, Britain had become its slave.

Yet for the student at the end of the twentieth century, Britain remains an important historical force in the shaping of American culture and society. From the foggy islands in the North Sea we have inherited a language, a literature with the world's best poetry and drama, and customs of civility and behavior. Sovereignty, we argue in common, resides with the people, not with the government, which in some parts of the world grandly refers to itself as "the State."

There is, however, a lesson for this country in the study of the period covered by this essay: the dangers to a nation as a result of lack of selfexamination, call it smugness. A central thesis of the essay has been the argument that Britain refused to recognize its altered place in the world after the Great War. Britain insisted upon continuing as the policeman of the world without assessing whether it had the resources to do so. The thoughtless guarantee to Poland, a piece of bluster, took Britain into the Second World War.

There may be a warning for the United States here. Certainly it would be false to argue that this country's economic condition is in any way analogous to Britain's in the 1920s and 1930s, but on the other hand, our obligations are infinitely larger, and the world is in ferment. With the poverty of many of the new nations, the enormous wealth possessed by the United States is itself a cause of ferment.

Finally, public opinion, the exercise of the popular sovereignty which we share with Britain and value highly, has today a dozen ways of forming opinions and making itself felt, ways that did not exist sixty years ago. The student must remember that appeasement was created, supported, and finally killed after Prague by British public opinion. The result was war, which the public emphatically did not want. Management of foreign policy by popular whim is rarely successful.

Today the huge influence of television, which can turn an isolated event, say a drought halfway around the world, into a foreign policy crisis, and public opinion polling, which can spur the nation's leaders to take action on matters they scarcely understand, makes the systematic planning of foreign affairs nearly impossible.

Britain lost the diplomatic initiative against Hitler in March 1936 when the British public responded to the invasion of the Rhineland with a yawn. Thereafter Chamberlain lurched from crisis to crisis—Austria, Sudetenland, Prague, Danzig, Poland—trying to improvise a policy, never catching up, but unable to exert any influence because of the public's paralysis from the fear of aerial bombardment. "Diplomacy without power," said Bismarck, "is like an orchestra without instruments." In a British or American democracy, public opinion and the media that control it are the source of power.

The lesson from the British experience for the United States today proceeds from its value as an illustration of the danger of allowing complex foreign policy decisions to be guided by public opinion. Today the problem is compounded. The channels for opinion formulation are multiplied. The American public is at once cynical and sentimental and easily moved to call for government action to interfere in some other nation's affairs. So far we have been fortunate if foolish. We have simply withdrawn, sometimes leaving the problem, whatever it was, unsolved, occasionally made worse, but we have not been hurt. We may not always be so lucky.

BIBLIOGRAPHICAL ESSAY

In this bibliography I do not attempt to provide a comprehensive reference for scholars, but rather a selection of books dealing with subjects discussed in the essay that may be of help to the undergraduate researcher. In addition I have suggested, on a few occasions warned about, useful books which should be used with care.

Among the many general histories of Britain in the twentieth century two which must be mentioned immediately as of enduring value are A. J. P. Taylor, *England 1914–45*, Oxford, 1965, and C. L. Mowat, *Britain Between the Wars, 1918–1939*, London, 1955. For the student of politics Mowat is to be preferred. It is more detailed and less afflicted by the quips and cocksure generalizations which Taylor seems unable to resist. Moreover Taylor's conclusions, on the war debt for example, are childish. On the other hand Taylor covers, albeit briefly, social, economic and cultural affairs as well as politics. An excellent textbook covering the first three-quarters of the century is Alfred Havighurst, *Britain in Transition*, Chicago, 1979. Another volume well worth consulting, particularly on foreign and imperial policy is W. N. Medlicott, *Contemporary England, 1914–64*, New York, 1967. Despite the terminal dates, easily three-quarters of the book concerns the interwar period.

Newer general works in the large and gloomy field of Britain's growing weakness in the first half of the twentieth century are Robert Blake, *The Decline of Power, 1914–1964*, New York, 1985; and on British politics and foreign affairs generally, David Reynolds, *Britannia Overruled, British Policy and World Power in the Twentieth Century*, London, 1991. Reynolds is to be preferred. Lord Blake's study shows signs of haste and is not quite what one would have expected from so distinguished a scholar.

On economics one can hardly do better than Sidney Pollard, *The Development of the British Economy, 1914–1950*, London, 1967 and later editions, and Derek Aldcroft, *The Inter-War Economy, Britain 1919–1939*, London, 1970. There are, of course, innumerable studies of narrower topics: unemployment, trade, finance, social evolution, and so on. For an important statistical analysis of British underinvestment central to this essay, see *The Economist*, October 24, 1992, "Down But Not Out," 20 pp. Among these, for the development of the welfare state see Bentley B. Gilbert, *British Social Policy, 1914–1939*, Ithaca, New York, 1970. A newer and briefer, but excellent, study is G. C. Peden, *British Economic and Social Policy: Lloyd George to Thatcher*, Atlantic Highlands, New Jersey, 1985. For social history, see John Stevenson, *British Society, 1914–1945*, London, 1984, a splendid volume; and Ronald Blythe, *The Age of Illusion, 1919–1940*, Oxford, 1983, a highly entertaining series of essays, some on trivia, some on transient sensations that filled the newspapers such as Edward VIII, and some on important topics, such as the fall of Neville Chamberlain. Robert Graves and Alan Hodge, *The Long Weekend*, London, 1940, remains a minor classic on British society between 1918 and 1939. It is still in print and widely used as a text. Finally, one must mention Corelli Barnett, *The Pride and the Fall*, New York, 1987. This is another book about decline, caused this time by the pernicious effect of Britain's still-existing Victorian social system upon industrial efficiency. Students should be warned that Barnett is always angry, and his opinions are by no means the last word. Nonetheless, this book has excited much comment.

THE GREAT WAR

Command and General Histories

There are histories without end of the Great War—political, strategic, tactical, economic, social, and diplomatic—but those intended for the beginning student often tend either toward unwarranted generalization or popular sensationalism. Probably the best single-volume study, still widely available, ideal for consultation and indeed for reading from cover to cover by the determined scholar, is Charles F. M. Cruttwell, *A History of the Great War*, Oxford, 1936. This is a general history written from a thoroughly English perspective by a professional scholar of military history at Oxford University who had served as well as a field officer in the conflict. For a modern work, combining a history of the war with a social study of the British army see J. M. Bourne, *Britain and the Great War, 1914–1918*, London, 1989. For a general textbook, one could recommend a Canadian writer, James L. Stokesbury, *A Short History of World War I*, New York, 1981.

On the military story of the Great War, a fierce and continuing debate which shows no signs of resolution has concerned the quality of British generalship. At the center of this controversy, but by no means alone, looms the figure of Field Marshal Douglas Lord Haig, First Earl Haig of Bemersyde, General Officer Commanding the British Expeditionary Force. The opening volley in this battle probably was fired by George A. B. Dewar and J. H. Boraston, *Sir Douglas Haig's Command*, 2 vols., London, 1922, written largely from Haig's despatches, and admitting no mistakes whatever by Haig. A violent denunciation of Haig followed in David Lloyd George's *War Memoirs*, 6 vols., Boston, 1933–1937. This huge work is often criticized as selfserving, which it is. Lloyd George does not admit many errors either. Yet, in attempting to defend himself, for example in explaining why he kept Haig as G.O.C. of the B.E.F. through the last two-and-one-half years of the war, Lloyd George prints hundreds of letters and confidential government documents that would otherwise be inaccessible to the undergraduate student. His six volumes are well worth consulting. The newest, perhaps most vitriolic, attack upon Haig appears in Denis Winter, *Haig's Command*, London, 1991. The student should remember that this book has elicited much critical comment. No researcher should neglect Robert Blake, ed., *The Private Papers of Douglas Haig, 1914–1919*, London, 1952. A recent defender of Haig is John Terraine, *Douglas Haig, The Educated Soldier*, London, 1963. On Haig and Rawlinson and military operations, see Robin Prior, *Command on the Western Front*, Oxford, 1992.

Special Topics

Two of the best brief sources on the causes of British participation in the Great War, not new but by men who could hardly
have been closer to the events described are Winston S.
Churchill, *The World Crisis*, Vol. I, New York, 1924, and H.
H. Asquith, *The Genesis of the War*, New York, 1923. The two
complement each other well. Indeed Asquith uses Churchill's
1912 speech to the Committee of Imperial Defence on British
naval redeployment as the basis of his explanation of that event.
Churchill's book contains also a widely reprinted and moving
account of his personal reflections in the final hours before the
declaration of war at 11:00 P.M. on August 4, 1914. For a sum-
mary of the story see Bentley B. Gilbert, "Pacifist to Interven-
tionist, David Lloyd George in 1911 and 1914. Was Belgium an
Issue?", *Historical Journal*, XXVIII, 4 (Dec. 1985), 863–85. See
also the very detailed Cameron Hazlehurst, *Politicians at War July
1914 to May 1915*, London, 1971.

On a critical, almost decisive, military event for Britain, the
undergraduate should read first Alan Moorehead, *Gallipoli*,
London, 1956, and second, Churchill, *World Crisis*, II. But he
should not neglect, if available, the highly controversial reports
of the Dardanelles Commission, Parliamentary Papers, 1917–
18, *Cds. 8490, 8902*, "Dardanelles Commission Preliminary Report," and P.P. 1919, *Cmd. 371*, "Final Report." These, particularly
the second, are severely critical of Asquith. The report was completed during Asquith's Prime Ministership. He declined to
publish it. Lloyd George, as Prime Minister, published in February 1917 a much censored Preliminary Report over Asquith's
strenuous objections. He allowed the Final Report to appear after
the Armistice. The two important modern biographies of Asquith
are Roy Jenkins, *Asquith*, London, 1964, which contained little
that was new except extracts from some of the letters to Venetia
Stanley while affirming that Jenkins worshiped Asquith. For a
newer, briefer, but more balanced assessment see Stephen Koss,
Asquith, London, 1976.

On Lloyd George during the war, in addition to his *War
Memoirs*, see Peter Rowland, *David Lloyd George, a Biography*, New
York, 1975. For the story of Lloyd George in the war to the end

of 1916 see also Bentley B. Gilbert, *David Lloyd George, a Political Life, 1912–1916*, Columbus, Ohio, 1992, II.

A basic source on the politics of the war—particularly the fall of Asquith, with the caveat that it constitutes a source, not a scholarly work—is W. M. Aitken, Lord Beaverbrook, *Politicians and the War, 1914–16*, London, 1960, and *Men and Power*, London, 1959. In the same category of historical memoir, too frequently overlooked, is Reginald, Viscount Esher, *The Tragedy of Lord Kitchener*, New York, 1921. Other important biographies are Robert Blake, *Unrepentant Tory, The Life and Times of Andrew Bonar Law*, New York, 1956; and Ian Colvin, *The Life of Lord Carson*, 3 vols., London, 1936. On Churchill, Henry Pelling, *Churchill*, London, 1974, would be preferable for the undergraduate. Indispensable on wartime politics is Stephen Roskill, *Hankey, Man of Secrets*, I, London, 1970; and David R. Woodward, *Lloyd George and the Generals*, Newark, Delaware, 1983.

For Ireland, a good clear introduction to the Easter Rising is Edgar Holt, *Protest in Arms*, New York, 1961.

On the two linked consecutive, overarching, but rather neglected issues of guns and men, the student should consult R. J. Q. Adams, *Arms and the Wizard, Lloyd George and the Ministry of Munitions, 1915–1916*, College Station, Texas, 1978; and R. J. Q. Adams and Philip Poirier, *The Conscription Controversy in Great Britain*, Columbus, Ohio, 1987.

Finally, on Britain's reaction to the war both at home and in the trenches, the big new book is Trevor Wilson, *The Myriad Faces of War*, London, 1985. This is close to being an encyclopedia of social evolution for the years 1914–18, but remains fascinating. Narrower and older, and oriented toward labor, is Arthur Marwick, *The Deluge, British Society and the First World War*, London, 1966.

Two semimemoirs, seminovels, in some ways the British equivalent of Remarque's *All Quiet on the Western Front*, all of which in fact were first published at the same time, at the height of the antiwar sentiment in the late twenties, are Siegfried Sassoon, *Memoirs of an Infantry Officer*, London, 1983; and Robert Graves, *Good-Bye to All That*, London, 1929. Perhaps Denis Winter's solid study of life in the British army trenches, *Death's*

Men, Soldiers of the Great War, London, 1978, should be read concurrently.

BETWEEN THE WARS

Special Topics, Politics

An excellent, lucid introduction to the story of Britain's participation at the peace conference in Paris is Harold Nicolson, *Peacemaking, 1919*, London, 1933. Nicolson was a member of the British delegation as was John Maynard Keynes whose commentary on the conference and the resulting Treaty of Versailles, *The Economic Consequences of the Peace*, New York, 1920, remains one of the few books of this century really to alter the thinking and voting of a large number of people. It also made Keynes a public figure. Written in sparkling prose, it should be required reading for the student of modern British, and indeed American, diplomatic and economic history.

On postwar politics, in addition to Taylor, Mowat, and Havighurst already cited, see Trevor Wilson, *The Downfall of the Liberal Party, 1914–1935*, London, 1966, which deals fully with the general election of 1918; and John Campbell, *Lloyd George, The Goat in the Wilderness*, London, 1977. The latter provides not only the story of Lloyd George's decline, but also a well-finished history of politics in the 1920s. For the more advanced student, Maurice Cowling, *The Impact of Labour, 1920–1924*, London, 1971, is worth consulting.

All of the previously mentioned books discuss the Irish troubles and the Treaty at some length, but for a special study see, Frank Pakenham, Lord Longford, *Peace by Ordeal*, London, 1935. For the British side of the Troubles, which has received much less attention, see D. G. Boyce, *Englishmen and Irish Troubles, British Public Opinion and the Making of Irish Policy, 1918–1922*, Cambridge, Mass., 1972.

Similarly the impact of the 1929–31 exchange crisis, the cost of unemployment, and the banking-political crisis of 1931 is treated in most general and economic histories. A well-informed special study may be found in Robert Skidelsky, *Politicians and the Slump, The Labour Government of 1929–1931*, London, 1968. On the core problem of unemployment insurance and on the exchange crisis see Gilbert, *Social Policy*. An excellent biography of MacDonald is David Marquand, *Ramsay MacDonald*, London, 1977. As has been noted there is no fully satisfactory biography of Baldwin. Keith Middlemas and John Barnes in *Stanley Baldwin*, London, 1969, have made a hugely ambitious attempt to define that elusive man, but had the misfortune to publish their study just as the fifty-year rule on official documents was suspended. For a succinct and impartial story of the royal abdication of 1936 see Frances Donaldson, *Edward VIII*, London, 1974.

On working-class life, in effect what it meant to be poor and out of work in Britain in the twenties and thirties, there are two enduring classics that no student should miss, Walter Greenwood, *Love on the Dole*, London, 1933, one of the truly great and far too rare novels about industrial life in the immediate postwar 1920s; and George Orwell, *The Road to Wigan Pier*, London, 1937, an angry report by a soon-to-be famous commentator on conditions during the mid-thirties in the depressed towns of the north of England.

APPEASEMENT, THE ORIGINS OF THE SECOND WORLD WAR

Telford Taylor, *Munich*, New York, 1979, provides far more than the story of the conference of September 29–30, 1938. It is, in fact, a massive and detailed account of British foreign policy in the 1930s. For undergraduates an excellent and new book is R. J. Q. Adams, *British Politics and Foreign Policy in the Age of Appeasement, 1935–39*, Stanford, 1993. An earlier, less detailed story, focusing on the political climate in Britain, is Martin Gilbert, *The Roots of Appeasement*, London, 1967. An easily available, almost forgotten source for Cabinet opinion on dealing with Hitler is Ian Colvin, *The Chamberlain Cabinet*, New York, 1971. This hastily thrown together collection of Cabinet documents was compiled when the fifty-year rule was modified. Nonetheless, it can be of considerable use to the undergraduate researcher. One should study, of course, the biographies of Neville Chamberlain, Keith Feiling, *The Life of Neville Chamberlain*, London, 1947; and Iain Macleod, *Neville Chamberlain*, London, 1961. For Chamberlain at the Ministry of Health, the first volume of a badly needed biography, see David Dilks, *Neville Chamberlain*, Cambridge, 1984.

On the political-military topic of appeasement, one problem is to find an individual willing to admit after the war that he had opposed the military coercion of Hitler. One such is B. H. Liddell Hart whose *Memoirs*, 2 vols., London, 1965, describe at length why he believed the British army should not be ordered to war in 1939. It provides as well his arguments through the previous two decades for improving the army. The student should be warned that Capt. Liddell-Hart today is a somewhat controversial figure who may not have been so influential as he believed himself to be. Nevertheless, he was an immensely well-informed military critic, and his memoirs are of great value to anyone looking for a candid assessment of the state of British land forces in the coming contest with Germany.

A second insider in the political world, the subject of an excellent recent biography, is Thomas Jones, an intimate of both Lloyd George and Baldwin, less so of Chamberlain, E. L. Ellis, *The Life of Thomas Jones*, Cardiff, 1992. In addition to this new biography the student should see Jones's own account of the thirties, *Diary With Letters, 1931–1950*, London, 1954. Jones opposed war because he felt Britain was not ready, politically, psychologically, or militarily. This was approximately the view of the Chamberlain Cabinet.

Given that the assignment of responsibility for the second war is a good deal easier than for the first, there have been a good many general histories of its origins. Beyond all doubt the best known, and probably most frequently criticized, is A. J. P. Taylor, *The Origins of the Second World War*, London, 1961. Like all of Taylor's books it is written with assertive confidence accompanied by striking conclusions that are too often designed to shock or surprise rather than to teach. A student new to the field should consult a more sober account, Keith Eubank, *The Origins of World War II*, Wheeling, Illinois, 1990.

THE SECOND WORLD WAR

General Histories and Command

There are, of course, many excellent general histories. Indispensable, obviously, is Winston Churchill's *The Second World War*,

6 vols., Cambridge, Massachusetts, 1946–53. These volumes are a delight to read, although to this writer they are more a badly organized memoir and less an explanation of the conflict than *The World Crisis*. Neither is a history, but both print many statistics and documents that otherwise would not be so easily available, as do Lloyd George's *Memoirs*. But like the Lloyd George story, the reader should remember that Churchill is providing also a vindication of his own behavior. Martin Gilbert's very full account of the war years, *Winston S. Churchill*, vols. VI and VII, London, 1983, 1986, offers some balance and much extra documentation, but is almost unreadable. The student could look at Arthur Bryant, *The Turn of the Tide* and *Triumph in the West*, New York, 1957, 1959. These books, supposedly a biography of Churchill's Chief of the Imperial General Staff, Allen Brooke, are in no sense a connected story but simply a stitching together of Lord Allenbrooke's diaries. Nonetheless they are very useful. Allenbrooke displays a good deal of polite exasperation about his chief. For more pungent comments on Churchill and an admiring picture of Chamberlain as well as an intimate study of Britain's wartime diplomacy, see David Dilks, ed., *The Diaries of Sir Alexander Cadogan, 1938–1945*, New York, 1972. A very full introductory history for the serious student, covering all theaters of the war, but written by Englishmen with a British and indeed Imperial perspective not too easily found is Peter Calvocoressi and Guy Wint, *Total War, The Causes and Courses of the Second World War*, London, 1972. An excellent newer book, again on the war in general but with a British point of view and providing, unusually, a mass of comparative statistical information on the combatants, on manufacturing capability, military resources, economic health, and so on, is R. A. C. Parker, *The Struggle for Survival, The History of the Second World War*, Oxford, 1989. One should consult also Henry Pelling, *Britain and the Second World War*, London, 1970. On the critical story of the Royal Navy in the second war, no one should miss Corelli Barnett, *Engage the Enemy More Closely*, London, 1991. This book provides an admirable study of Royal Navy operations on all oceans with the usual Barnett denunciation of a system that sent gallant men into battle with inferior equipment. Among the many works on the Battle of Britain, most accessible as a reference, is still Derek Wood and Derek Dempster, *The Narrow*

Margin, The Battle of Britain and the Rise of Air Power, rev. ed., New York, 1969. This is an excellent tool for undergraduate research, providing hard facts rather than sensational accounts of air battles. It contains the Order of Battle for both the R.A.F. and the *Luftwaffe*, and a valuable daily diary of events as well as useful statistics, both British and German. On Churchill's conduct of the war and his sometimes painful relations with the military, both British and American, an excellent short book is Barrie Pitt, *Churchill and the Generals*, London, 1981. The latest book on Churchill, highly revisionist and controversial, marked by many mistakes of fact on his earlier career, is John Charmley, *Churchill: The End of Glory*, London, 1993.

POLITICS AND SOCIETY AT HOME

Although Churchill's *Second World War* provides some insight into domestic politics between 1939 and 1945, the indispensable account appears in Paul Addison, *The Road to 1945, British Politics and the Second World War*, London, 1975. This is mainly an explanation in depth of how Labour won the general election of 1945. A useful supplement is A. J. P. Taylor, *Beaverbrook*, London, 1972, which is also worth consulting on the administrations of Lloyd George and Stanley Baldwin. On civilian life during the war, drawing on a variety of public opinion measuring services, see Angus Calder, *The People's War, 1939–45*, London, 1969. For an accurate picture of popular detachment and irresolution in the first year of the war, written with hilarious irony see Evelyn Waugh's novel, *Put Out More Flags*, London, 1942.

On the impact of the war upon social services the basic book is Richard Titmuss's volume in the civil history series, *Problems of Social Policy*, Her Majesty's Stationery Office, London, 1950 and, in the same field, on W. H. Beveridge and his report, W. H. Beveridge, *Power and Influence*, New York, 1955. This is a remarkably candid and at times amusing account of a career in government service that began with Churchill and Lloyd George and ended with Churchill. See also José Harris, *William Beveridge, A Biography*, Oxford, 1977.

On the special topic of Americans in Britain within a growing literature see Juliet Gardiner, *Overpaid, Oversexed, & Over Here, The American GI in World War II Britain*, London, 1992.

Britain, 1914–1945 includes many, perhaps too many, statistics, but statistics, honestly used, constitute strong historical evidence. The essential source for British numerical data that no historian can afford to be without is B. R. Mitchell and Phyllis Dean, *Abstract of British Historical Statistics*, Cambridge, 1962. A second source, much used in this essay, is *British Labour Statistics, 1886–1968*, Her Majesty's Stationery Office, London, 1971. Appropriately, this official publication cites Mitchell and Dean as the source for some of its tables.

The ultimate source for all late nineteenth- and twentieth-century demographic, commercial and government statistics is the official series, two volumes of which have been used in this essay, Board of Trade, "Statistical Abstract for the United Kingdom for each of the fifteen years from 1911 to 1925," P.P., 1927, *Cmd. 2849*; and Board of Trade, "Statistical Abstract for each of the fifteen years 1913 and 1924 to 1937," P.P., 1939, *Cmd. 5903*.

Finally, no one can hope to work in twentieth century British political history without having at his elbow the latest edition of David Butler and Gareth Butler, *British Political Facts, 1900–1985*, Macmillan, London, 1986.

INDEX

About the Author: Bentley Brinkerhoff Gilbert is Professor of History at the University of Illinois at Chicago. He is the author of *Evolution of National Insurance in Great Britain, Britain Since 1918, British Society Policy,* and *David Lloyd George: A Political Life,* Volume II of which won the Society of Midland Authors Prize for Biography in 1993.